Petticoats to Pitchforks

Terry Finnamore

First published 2004
Edward Gaskell publishers
6 Grenville Street
Bideford
Devon
EX39 2EA

isbn 1-898546-68-1

Petticoats to Pitchforks

Terry Finnamore

Printed and bound by
Lazarus Press
Unit 7 Caddsdown Business Park
Bideford
Devon EX39 3DX
www.lazaruspress.com

This book is dedicated to my husband John
and all our wonderful family.

Also to Joan Squire for all her hard work typing it.

Author's Note

The Women's Land Army was first formed in 1917 during the First World War.

In June 1939, with the threat of the Second World War looming, the organisation was again formed with the result that by September 1939, when the call came, a thousand volunteers could immediately be sent into employment, many of them already trained.

I was born Beatrice Leake, and in the Land Army was always known as Titch. This later changed to Terry, and this name has stayed with me to this day.

My story begins in 1946 and continues until the WLA was disbanded in 1950. During these years 80% of home grown food went to feed the British public.

FOREWORD

Beginning in Warwickshire, and then moving to North Devon, this book gives a different slant on the lives of those who joined the Women's Land Army at the end of the War, and served until it was finally disbanded.

Most books depict the stories of girls living on private farms one or two at a time, whereas this is about the ones who lived in close proximity in hostels or large Nissen huts; forty or more at a time going to different farms in small gangs each day.

It tells the tales of farmers, the methods of farming in those days, of animals and their funny ways, and of working with POWs who had not yet been sent back home to Germany; really amusing stories of the nights out mixing with the local people, the workers and joining in the town's celebrations.

Everything in this book is a first hand account of those wonderful years written by one of the girls who loved the life as many others did and has remained in North Devon, never forgetting how it really was.

CHAPTER ONE

It was just another ordinary day and I was walking through the ward answering yet another call for "bed pan please, nurse". Glancing at the sunshine outside, I remembered looking out of the classroom window as a child at an inner city school, longing to be running through green fields, feeling as free as air. Out of the blue the thought came to me; time for a change.

To this day I cannot say why, as I loved both my work and lifestyle at that time, but the idea had formed and there would be no going back.

Looking into possible outdoor careers I finally found the answer, little knowing the choice I was to make would be the beginning of some of the happiest days of my life – as a Land Girl in the Women's Land Army.

At the interview a few weeks later, I was told that if a medical examination proved me fit I would be accepted. My doctor laughingly told me he would pass me if I sent him a few eggs and some cream from the first farm I went to. I made him no firm promise on this.

Sitting on the bus going to the railway station, I reflected over the past month: Having to collect my uniform, saying farewell to my stepmother and small sister, the sadness I felt at leaving behind good friends I had lived and worked with during the past year, walking in the hospital grounds in the summer evenings, savouring the air around me, looking to the future with excited anticipation. Waking from my reverie I realised I had arrived at the station with little time to spare. The train was already waiting.

CHAPTER TWO

My dash along the platform halted when a compart-
ment door was thrown open, someone shouted,
"Quick, in here," and a pair of hands pulled me
aboard. Glancing around I saw several friendly faces smiling
at me. Girls dressed as I was; the heavy khaki greatcoat,
breeches held in by long socks, well polished shoes, neat shirt
with green tie, and lastly the hat with the wheatsheaf WLA
badge on front. I also found to my sheer joy that we were all
bound for the same destination, Leamington Spa, our first
posting.

We exchanged names during the journey, and found we all
came from the Midlands. To add to the camaraderie, we
decided it would be good fun to have nicknames. Tibs,
Jeannie and Ginger, were to remain friends and room-mates.
Sheila, the youngest member, became Babs, and we were to
become close friends, visiting each other's homes when on

leave. My five-foot one-inch frame inevitably landed me as Titch.

The cheerful driver waiting for us at the station soon loaded us and our luggage into an open-backed lorry. We were strangely quiet travelling the nine miles along Banbury road, watching the fields and hedges go by, no doubt wondering how we would cope with our new life. Would we still be here after our ten week probationary period was over? Only time would tell.

Arriving at the camp we found there were half a dozen Nissen huts standing on the outskirts of a deserted airfield. A short distance away there were two more where a handful of Air Force men had been left behind to clear the stores.

The lorry came to a halt. Waiting to welcome us, the warden, who was in sole charge of the welfare of all the girls, guided us to our sleeping quarters. These seemed very bare and gloomy as we went inside; there were ten old iron beds with folded mattresses and blankets, a tall locker beside each one. A stove stood in the middle of the room. The warden told us to unpack and make the beds, and she would send someone to fetch us for the evening meal.

There was a great deal of laughter and good natured teasing as we settled ourselves. Deciding to wash and change into civvy clothes, we found the toilets and showers in a large galvanised hut, unheated of course, across a long stretch of grass. We guessed it was going to be no picnic on chilly early mornings, or for a quick dash in the middle of the night.

The someone who had been sent to fetch us was Dora, a rather bossy individual who gave us a long lecture on all the "do's and don'ts". We found out later she had only been there a week herself.

Walking into the dining room, it was a pleasant surprise to find one area had been turned into a cosy communal lounge with brightly painted murals of girls working in the fields adorning the tops of the walls. These murals were beautifully done by German prisoners of war who worked for the Air Force during the day before going back to the internment camp at night. On hearing the Land Girls were moving in, they had decorated the walls as a welcoming gesture.

While we waited at the long bare tables for the meal to start, the door burst open and suddenly the room was filled with muddy, dishevelled girls laughing and shouting to each other. The serving hatch lifted with a loud bang, a queue formed and each girl picked up a plate already loaded with food. The new arrivals, including myself, waited until all the other girls had been served and then quietly collected ours.

My mind went back to the nurses' homes. The starched white table cloths, good silver cutlery, pleasant maids who had waited on us while the stern faced sisters at a separate table checked our table manners and good behaviour which was expected at all times. I was brought back to reality by someone saying "Are you going to eat all that, Titch?" I shook my head and the girl took my plate, scooped the remains on to hers and continued to eat with gusto. Shrugging off thoughts of the niceties of life, I thought 'oh well, you're here now, water under the bridge and all that,' and went to the hatch and grabbed a mug of tea.

The long evening stretched ahead; there was no television in those days, just the radio and endless conversation. Then a message came from the Air Force lads to say they were taking their lorry into town and would give us a lift, if we could get the nine-thirty bus back. Only the girls who had joined that day decided to go.

We had a pleasant time in town, drank tea in the NAFFI, chatted to the regulars there, and eventually found our way back to the bus. This bus was run for the convenience of the soldiers at the barracks, four miles from our camp, and we were to make good use of it in the coming months.

We crept quietly into the hut so as not to disturb the other girls and found getting into our beds was impossible. The others had been busy in our absence making apple pie beds. We knew the culprits were still awake as we could hear giggling coming from across the room; mayhem followed as pillows flew in all directions and girls were forcibly tipped out of bed. Dora tried to shout above the din something that sounded like, "... seeing the warden about all this in the morning".

The daily routine was the same every working day: after rising at six o'clock, have a quick wash and then dress in shirt, bib-and-brace dungarees, green jumper, gum boots and three-quarter length cloth cow coat. Breakfast was egg and bacon or something on toast. Food was still rationed so we had only six slices of bread, one ounce of butter and one ounce of cheese which we made into sandwiches for packed lunch.

Work rotas were placed on the wall by the work supervisor. These showed a list of names under the headings of the farms employing us. Sometimes there were groans of "oh no, not there again," when a farm visited before was not very popular. Also listed was the van or lorry we were to ride in, with strict instructions to be loaded up by seven o'clock.

My first day was spent picking potatoes. A tractor with a spinner attached tossed the potatoes over the open ground and two girls to a measured patch gathered them into a wooden basket; one girl held the sack and the other tipped the potatoes in. There was hardly time to do this before the tractor was creeping up on us again. In a large field there were as many as fourteen girls to a row.

During the morning the farmer's wife brought out a jug of tea for our ten minute break. She also did this for the dinner hour at one o'clock. We ate our food along with the mud we hadn't managed to rub off onto our trousers. A dash behind a hedge served as a toilet.

The long afternoon dragged on until the lorry arrived at five o'clock. As we bumped along the lane leading out of the farm I wondered how many of my muscles had been severely damaged. I consoled myself with the fact that a hot meal would be waiting; I had eaten all my sandwiches at the first break and was absolutely starving.

The next few weeks are difficult to recall, trying to come to terms with all the varied hard work which was part of farm life. Muck spreading was good fun – once you ignored the smell. The tractor drove slowly round the field with us standing on the trailer forking dung into heaps at intervals ready to be scattered with wild abandon over the ground.

Threshing corn was one of the jobs I liked best. The thresher was a huge machine driven by a belt from a traction engine standing beside the rick. We usually had a team of four girls; one stood on the rick tossing sheaves onto the top of the thresher to the second girl who would cut the bands, shaking the sheaves into a large drum which separated the corn from the straw. The third girl stood at the back taking off the tied up straw, pitching it to a man who would stack it, making another rick. The fourth girl, beneath the machine, would be raking out the husks onto sheets of sacking. This particular job was very traumatic, the dust and dirt are hard to imagine; with a scarf covering your mouth to prevent choking, clothes and skin covered in grime, it was hard to see as it flew into your eyes. We all changed places during the day to get relief from this.

The rewards were great, however. At dinner time all the crew ambled into the farmhouse kitchen where a roast meal was waiting followed by apple tart and cream, all washed down with mugs of steaming hot tea.

No matter how tired we were at the end of the day, we always managed to sing. As the lorry did the rounds picking up each gang from different farms, they automatically joined in.

As the weather turned colder and the tasks became more difficult – digging out muddy ditches, threading wires through a baler all day in high open fields, feeling your hands going numb with the cold, many girls got discouraged. As many as fifteen left in one week, cancelling their contracts. The girls left behind were told to pack all our belongings by the weekend. We were moving to other quarters.

CHAPTER THREE

Our new home was a large house standing on a hill and with its own grounds. It was only a couple of miles from our old camp but sheer luxury after the huts. We looked excitedly around the rooms deciding who would sleep where.

Tibs and company chose a room for three up the back stairs – probably the servants' quarters in better times. Norma, Nona and four others chose an upstairs room, as did the others, finding places where friends could be together. Dora, Nora, Mary, Moira, Jean, Babs and myself took the downstairs room. One large window looked down onto the main road, the other faced the drive leading up to the front door. The warden's quarters in the next room was attached to the large hall which served as a dining room. Adjoining this was a spacious lounge with a large marble fireplace. We still had the same beds and lockers but who cared, the showers and toilets were inside.

As it was Saturday we were debating whether to go to the cinema in town that evening when a call came through from the army camp inviting us all to a dance at the barracks that night. Unless we had a special pass we always had to be in by ten thirty, but as a special treat this time we were allowed to be out until midnight. The army had laid on transport to fetch us and bring us back at the end of the evening. It was a great night out, everyone went out of their way to make us welcome. The dance was held in the main hall, the band played up-to-the-minute music. Babs, who was a really attractive girl, was soon surrounded by admirers. There was a power cut and we thought that was the end of the evening, but the army had other ideas. Two motor bikes were ridden in and we carried on dancing with the aid of the headlights. We were invited to the camp's weekly dances from then on. Lying in bed, the girls swapped stories of the evening out. Most had arranged to meet someone during the week.

At the back of the house stood a bike rack containing about a dozen bikes which had seen better days. If any farms were less that three miles away, we had to cycle. Knowing only a couple of these bikes were rideable, there was always a dash to get them first.

Riding down the hill one morning, I decided to see how fast I could go without touching the brakes. It was so exhilarating, but I left it a little late to slow down – no brakes! I shot across the main road, two cars were driving towards me in each direction. I landed in the roadside ditch as they passed. Luckily for me I only had a few bruises, but the rack was missing one bike.

The week before Christmas saw us in a field pulling mangolds. These are something like a large swede, used for cattle feed. Tugging these from the ground, we topped and tailed them with a billhook and left them in heaps for the farmer to collect and store. Sometimes the ground was frozen, and the mangolds had to be booted out of the soil. There was half and hour to go before home time. I brought the hook down to find I had taken a slice from the top of my finger. Babs grabbed a scarf to wrap it, and hurried me to the farmhouse. Waiting for the farmer's wife to bring a bowl of water, Babs kept reassuring me I would be alright. As I plunged my hand into the water, the blood poured out and she promptly fainted. I looked at her in astonishment. My hand had been so cold I hadn't felt a thing.

Enjoying ourselves at the sergeants' mess seasonal festivities at the army camp, we all bought raffle tickets. Dora was asked to dance, and told me to hold onto her tickets. I won a bottle of whisky. Arriving back in our room, she accused me of taking her numbers. I was so annoyed at this I shared the whisky with anyone willing to drink it. Hardly anyone in the house had drunk alcohol before and only few decided to have a go. It took a lot of coughing and spluttering to get it down, and the room started to look very weird.

During the night I dreamt I was trying to get out of a pit, and awoke to find myself attempting to climb up the side of the locker.

Next morning was unreal. My image loomed towards me in the mirror, my legs didn't want to support me. I spied my fellow sufferers struggling to come to terms with the simple task of getting dressed. The warden, with the best of intentions, told us she had ordered a special breakfast. We stared at the kippers lying innocently on our plates and decided to report sick. We snuggled blissfully back into bed, but not for long. Somehow the warden had found out what had happened and she ordered us out of bed at the double to clean and polish the house. As I went out of the door I had a suspicion that she was trying to hide a smile.

The travel warrants had arrived. We were allowed four a year, and it was good to be going home for Christmas – the first leave since joining. Cheerful farewells were said at the station. Arriving home mid-afternoon, I stepped off the bus to be met by my young sister who had been sitting on a wall waiting since early morning. Christmas was quiet but very enjoyable. My stepmother remarked at the change in me; I seemed to have lost the ladylike manner I'd had while nursing. I tried to explain I'd needed to change a little to survive the rough working life I now had.

Two days after Boxing Day saw a return to duty. I was more than happy to be back, and welcoming voices greeted me as I walked into the lounge. I joined the girls there and curled up in a chair listening to the tales of everyone while on leave. A warm feeling of contentment swept through me.

It was not often we were sent out to do work which seemed a sheer waste of time, but this day was exceptional. A farmer owned fields at the far end of the army camp and wanted the stubble which was left from the summer to be harvested and scraped into mounds. The ground was covered in large patches of frozen ice and towards the end of the day, to relieve the boredom, we stuck our pitchforks into it and jumped up and down to see who could make the highest jet of water spurt up. Finding this great fun, I took an extra high jump, the ice cracked and I fell into a rut and was soaked to the waist in freezing cold water. Someone suggested I go back to the guard room and one girl took off her socks for me to wear, carrying my wet ones dangling from the pitchfork over her shoulder. I sat shivering in the guard room for an hour before the lorry came.

New Year's eve found me in the sick bay. Despite the warden's swift action in ordering a hot bath, a good meal and sending me straight to bed, I had woken next day with a sore throat and chill. The doctor arrived and advised a couple of days' rest. Feeling very sorry for myself I heard the girls going out to celebrate while I passed the time reading. I also heard their noisy return before the house settled down for the night. Or so I thought! At five minutes to midnight my small room was filled with girls, streamers and balloons covering my bed, and a lusty chorus of *Old Lang Syne* rang out. The horrified warden rushed in, shooed them out and wished me a Happy New Year. I lay there thinking how remarkable it was that each girl cared so much for the other.

I will not dwell too long in detail of what happened a few days later, all I know is that it was the most dreadful day in our Land Army lives. Everyone had gone to work in the morning discussing what to wear to the dance that night. During the morning we were rained off and phoned for transport to fetch us home as usual on such days. We were cleaning the house when three girls burst in screaming hysterically. It appears that Norma had been cutting bands on top of the thresher when she slipped into the revolving drum which had torn off her leg. We were all totally distraught at this awful news.

The warden came to us in her calm way that evening and insisted we went out as planned, and told us to try and shut the thoughts from our minds. In her wisdom she realised we would be sent out to tackle that same job the next day.

We made many enquiries and were kept well informed of Norma's progress, but all our requests to visit were refused;

quite understandable under the circumstances, but we would have loved to have given her all our support which she must have needed at that time.

After a long stay in hospital, Norma returned to live with her mother, her Land Army days were over. We heard nothing more.

During February it started to snow. We were granted short weekend leave from Saturday until Sunday night to allow us to see our families. I spent the first night at home, travelling next morning across Birmingham to spend the day with Babs in order to get the train back that night. We started out earlier than planned as the weather had worsened.

Back in Leamington we met four more of our friends who told us no vehicles could travel on the road. We made our way to the YMCA, asking to be put up there for the night. They refused, saying it was against the rules to take women in overnight, however we were welcome to use the phone to contact the warden to tell her of our plight. She asked to speak to the manager, pleading with him to find us somewhere to sleep, making herself responsible. We were offered a basement floor and blankets to lie on. The warden told us it was imperative to try to get back somehow in the morning because a farmer on a smallholding desperately needed help to thresh a small rick to use as bedding for his animals.

We set off at six o'clock next morning to walk the seven miles back, struggling to avoid the huge snowdrifts, picking the easiest paths we could find, laughing at our efforts to haul ourselves up when we fell. Four hours later we arrived. Praising our efforts, the warden told us to change our wet clothes, have breakfast and rest for an hour.

The farm was only one and a half miles away. Luckily the field with the rick adjoined the main road and the thresher which had been placed there before the snow came, was just inside the gate. The farmer was contacted to say we were on our way, and he and two men set to work digging their way into the gate to allow the tractor through. The snow was cleared and the tarpaulin from the rick and thresher removed. I worked up top feeding the machine – this was a job I liked and I had learned to do it with great speed.

We completed the work in three hours, then trudged our way home leaving behind a very grateful, happy farmer. Looking back it had been a marathon task; we accepted it as just another day.

Gradually the roads were cleared and the rest of the girls returned. We had many rest days as the only work we could do was at nearby farms, usually sorting potatoes which were piled against the wall in a barn. Kneeling in front of the heap they were sorted into three baskets – one type for eating, another for seed, and lastly the not so good ones for the pigs.

One farm we worked on had straw bales at the back of a barn. As the bales were removed and the heap diminished, dozens of rats ran out and through the open door, scattering in all directions. So did we! I ended up sitting on a gate watching the rats rush underneath. Definitely a job for the rat catcher there.

Working with animals made you feel good, especially those gentle giants the cart-horses. Their patience and obedience soon made you lose any fear felt on approaching them. One particular day the farmer was preparing the ground for seed sowing using a drag harnessed to the horse. He suggested it would be easier for me to ride while he walked behind freeing the drag from any obstruction. Sitting astride, using a sack as a saddle, we plodded up and down the field at a steady pace, turning at the hedges as we came to them. I felt like a real cowboy. At lunchtime I was told to give the horse a drink from the trough. As the horse's head went down, the collar slipped and slid down his neck, and I followed. Still hanging on grimly, I called for help. The farmer coming to my assistance curled up with laughter. I must have looked really ridiculous.

By the end of the afternoon my rump was feeling the worse for wear so I was relieved to start riding the horse back to the yard. What I didn't know was a horse can always sense when he is homeward bound. The stable was in sight, and without me having to lead him, his pace quickened almost to a trot, completely ignoring the fact that I was still on his back. The door was much lower than my head and I just managed to duck as we went in. I admit I was shaking just a little as I eased myself off, but the day had been a wonderful new experience and I had thoroughly enjoyed it.

Talk about naive, that's just what I was.

About a dozen of us went to the Officers Mess at the army camp after a request from them to help entertain a small group of young officers from Poland. The first man to enter the room caused quite a stir among the girls; he was very handsome with blond hair, very blue eyes and was not too tall. I wondered which girl he would ask to dance with, but having always considered myself a 'Plain Jane' compared to some of the other girls, I soon lost interest, however, a short while later he stood in front of me and asked for a dance. To the envy of all the other girls he continued to dance with me for most of the evening. He was very charming but rather shy.

Towards the end of the evening I asked if he would like to go and have something to eat. He followed me from the room into the dark outside and walked past a couple of store huts with all the windows blacked out. I opened the door to one of these and there were tables laden with food. He said, "There really is food." I smiled and said that yes of course there was and started to eat. Then, like a bolt from the blue it struck me, what did he *think* I had taken him out for?

Filled with embarrassment, I dashed out of the door and climbed into the truck waiting to take us home. The girls piled in and I told them what had happened. Suddenly there came a voice from outside the truck calling, pleading, "Teech, Teech," – which I suppose was Polish for Titch – "please meet me on Sunday." Despite the pleas of the girls to go out and speak to him, I firmly declined. Naive I may have been, but I still had my pride.

Spring in the countryside was beautiful. The wild daffodils opening out along the river banks, primroses in the hedgerows, young lambs calling incessantly to their mothers, whose deeper tones never failed to answer back.

It was then we met the Barford Boys, seven or eight farm lads from a village nearby. They started calling at the house to see if anyone wished to go out. There was no pairing up of couples, just a group of youngsters full of fun and enjoying good company. We would walk down to the inn at Ashorne village and sit around talking and laughing about some of the more amusing events of the day. I loved to study a picture on the wall – very simple, just a bread board holding a cottage loaf, a bread knife, beside this a piece of cheese and an onion. It looked so real, you could imagine yourself eating it.

These evenings which we found so relaxing all too soon came to an end. Haymaking had begun which meant long working hours, especially for the lads, to get the hay in while the weather held good. The work was very satisfying. Grass was cut and left in rows, we turned this to help it dry out, then along came the hay rake to scoop it into mounds. We loaded this into trailers or horse and cart, following the full load to wherever it was to be stacked. It was fed into a large conveyor while we stood underneath spreading it to form a rick. The smell of the hay was sweeter than any perfume you could buy.

People tend to look on pigs as rather mindless animals who go around nuzzling the ground and eating everything in sight. This second part may be right, but each pig has its own personality and are certainly not stupid.

When I first met Herbert, I sort of ignored him as he stood in the compound. Then I noticed that every time I walked past he grunted loudly as if trying to attract my attention. Mentioning this to the farmer, he told me that the pig was just a spoilt old boar who loved to have his back scratched, in fact it had become quite an obsession with him.

For the rest of that week I spent my breaktime sitting on the wall while Herbert leaned against it in a daze of ecstasy as I ate my lunch with one hand and, using a rough stick, scratched his back with the other.

On the nights we stayed in, we did our washing or ironing and then sat in the lounge playing cards, reading or listening to the radio. One evening the conversation turned to the good things we had in our home towns. This started off quite amiably until one girl said, "I think we have better shops in Birmingham than Coventry or Nottingham." Talk about waving a red rag in front of a bull, each girl in turn started to defend her own territory, pointing out what they had better than the other. Then it got really ridiculous with everyone shouting to drown out the other. Feeling I wasn't being heard and wanting to express my opinion further, I climbed on a chair in order to stand on the wide topped marble fireplace. Just as I was really getting into my stride, the warden came in and suddenly there was silence. She ordered me to get down, saying that from the noise, she had thought we were all being massacred. What a spoilsport; we had been thoroughly enjoying ourselves. After she had gone we all collapsed in our chairs and laughed until we cried.

The place we went to work at next was rather run down and we were clearing docks and weeds from a small plot. The owner was a very surly man who gave the impression he was doing us a favour employing us. It was apparent he lived alone. At morning break he brought our tea out in an old rusty can and there was a film of oil floating on top and it smelt strongly of paraffin. We told him it was undrinkable. He replied if it was good enough for him it was good enough for the likes of us. We were rather angry at this treatment, and knowing there was a small cafe not far along the road, we went there in our dinner hour. None of us had any money with us and so we explained things to the owner and asked if she would supply us with tea and trust us to send her the money. She evidently knew the man well as she readily agreed, and said she would be sending the bill straight to him.

There was a strict rule laid down that should there be a valid complaint against a farmer, by any girl working for him, he would be blacklisted, unable to employ us again. I must hasten to add that most farmers were caring and considerate people and this was the only time, to my knowledge, that this actually happened.

Bernard and I met on the nine thirty bus. He was a soldier from the camp, and had evidently noticed me on several occasions but had been too shy to ask me out. Babs sat beside him one night on the crowded bus. Realising she was my friend, he asked her to introduce him to me, if I agreed. I gave it a bit of thought and said I couldn't see why not.

He was a very pleasant looking lad, fair with blue eyes. We had many nice evenings out, going to the cinema or sometimes he called at the hostel and we went for walks, on occasions meeting at the camp dances. He asked if I would visit his home with him on my next leave, but I declined. He only had a few months of National Service left and wanted me to write to him when he went home and join him there later. I told him as gently as possible that I had no intention of settling down with anyone for a long time yet as I was happy as I was. He was such a nice person, I was so happy that we remained the best of friends whenever we met.

Warm summer sun had ripened the corn ready for harvesting. We stood around waiting for the tractor to start up and pull the binder which both cut and tied the corn into sheaves. Our job was to pick these up and place them bottom down into stooks of eight, leaning against each other with the ears (mostly barley or oats) looking upward to finish drying off. Rain at this time was the farmer's nightmare. Should the corn be put away damp, it turned to mildew and a whole season's work and profit would be gone.

As the binder neared the middle of the field, the farmworkers took their places around this area waiting for the rabbits to come out, running everywhere. Then the fun started; chasing after them, the faster we ran, the faster they ran. Needless to say, most of them got away, but the ones that were caught were fat and healthy – they had after all devoured a good quarter of the corn they were now running away from. There were many days of this; it has to be remembered, any work done on one farm was repeated by us dozens of times as we went from farm to farm.

Unfortunately I didn't finish the harvesting that year. It was discovered I had a hernia and was booked into a hospital in Birmingham to have this repaired. I travelled there alone but called in to see Babs' mother as it was on the way. It was very remiss of me, but I didn't write home to tell my family, I suppose my main thought was to just go and get it all over. When I came round from the anaesthetic, my stepmother was beside me. Evidently the hospital had asked the police to call and inform her as some paper or other had to be signed. I apologised for my lack of thought, but she was pleased I was alright. Bernard had sent me flowers and fruit. I really appreciated his thoughtfulness.

Five days later I was taken to a convalescent home at Bournville to recover for a couple of weeks. I went home for a short leave, then returned to Leamington to pack my bags. The Land Army Benevolent Fund was to pay for a two week recovery holiday at their rest home in Torquay, Devon.

The journey down seemed incredibly long. I watched the landscape change from the flatness of the Midlands to the hills and valleys of the South West. I had been told to hire a taxi to get to the hostel. Driving through the town I found it a really beautiful place; clean white hotel buildings, flowers seemed to be growing everywhere. Three Navy ships were at anchor paying a courtesy visit to the town. I stared at them in awe, I had never seen anything like this before.

I was made very welcome on my arrival at the hostel. It was much the same as any large guest house, spacious and comfortable, but at first I felt at a loss to be in a houseful of people who didn't know me. I missed all my friends and just wished I could be back amongst them. This didn't last too long however, as Land Army girls seemed to have the ability to mix in together wherever they were. Sometimes a few of us went into the town in the evenings. Looking around there were plenty of things to see there, but as our pocket money was only ten shillings a week, it didn't go far. The working wage stopped after so many weeks, so this was just a retainer. In any case we had to be in by nine o'clock as we were still in convalescent care. It was pleasant, and I loved the area.

The two weeks soon came to an end. Once again I was on the train looking forward to getting back to normal working life, but I knew then that if my plans took shape, I would be starting my way down yet another road.

My friends were delighted to see my return, and I was soon back into the swing of things. Deciding to have a quiet talk with Babs, we sat out on the lawn in front of the house. I told her all about Torquay, how lovely the Devonshire countryside was, and that I had decided to put in for a transfer to go there. She was really taken by surprise at this statement and thought I was joking. Then she asked me to wait before applying whilst she made a visit to her mother that weekend. If her family agreed, she would apply for a transfer with me. I was overjoyed, although I had already written home. I also decided to go home that weekend. All parties agreed. It seemed we were on out way to a new adventure.

CHAPTER FOUR

Our request for a transfer was for the Torbay area, so it was surprising that when the posting finally arrived it was for Torrington in North Devon. Leaving Leamington that morning, our written instructions told us to change trains at Exeter St Davids to the Southern Railway Line. We did this, and one and a half hours later we reached a place called Barnstaple where the train divided. The first carriages went on to Ilfracombe while the last two carriages were coupled up to another engine to continue our journey. It was getting quite dark and we thought we'd never get there. Approaching a well lit town we said, "This must be the place; doesn't look too bad", but no, the sign said Bideford. The next stop was our destination at last. Walking around the engine we saw the train could go no further. It was indeed the end of the line.

A small country bus was waiting at the station entrance with a few people on it. The overhead racks would just about hold a folded newspaper, and our jokey comments on this seemed to amuse the other passengers.

Alighting from the bus we found ourselves in the middle of a square; we were evidently in the town centre, but it was so deserted we thought it was a ghost town. Eventually we saw a lone inhabitant and we asked the way to the hostel. For certain he knew what he was saying, but the broad Devon accent was foreign to us, so we just went in the direction his finger was pointing. After much trial and error, and a mile walk, our suitcases getting heavier by the minute, we found it.

The hostel was a large L-shaped corrugated building with a low wall surrounding it, the front of the building spanned a long length of road. Entering the gate, we found the entrance door and went in. It was really nice inside with a communal lounge and dining room. The warden was pleased we had managed the difficult journey, apologising that the kitchen was closed for a hot meal but she could provide us with a snack and drink.

We walked into a small corridor. To our left were the washrooms, opposite these were the sleeping quarters. On each side of the long hut were cubicles holding two double bunk beds to sleep four in each partition. There was not a great deal of spare room as lockers were placed in there too. The other girls greeted us warmly. They had already made our beds for us, then came and sat beside the fire in the lounge, asking questions in order to find out all about us, saying we would meet the others when they came in from their evening out. I felt at home right away.

It took a little time to get my bearings next morning. I had taken the bottom bunk and wondered what the large bulk above my head was, then realised it had to be Babs. At breakfast I found out the main difference between this hostel and the last: Whereas the girls there had been from one area, here they came from all over the country; London, Liverpool, as far away as Newcastle, about 40 girls in all.

A happy thought struck me; it was Saturday, only half a day to work. Although the two of us did not really have to start duties until Monday, when asked, Babs and I agreed to be sent out. Babs went out with a gang on the lorry while I went to a nearby farm with a girl called Brenda.

It was pleasant walking along the road in the early morning. We stopped to sit on a small bridge to watch a stream running under the road. Turning into the lane, we saw the farmer loading his churns on the stand ready for the milk lorry to collect. The dairy factory was built into a valley at the other end of town.

The farmer gave us a lift down the road, asking us to clean out the shippen as the cows had already been let out into the fields. Inside, the place had an aroma all its own, the warm smell of the beasts that had just left mingling with the sweet scent of milk and hay.

We scrubbed at the floors with the large yard brooms, hosing down afterwards. All children love playing with water, and I was no exception. We spent the rest of the morning talking together whilst cleaning out the surrounding animal houses, with a leisurely stroll back to the hostel at dinner time.

On Saturday nights everyone went out into the town, where the only entertainment was the Saturday night dance in the drill hall – and thirteen pubs. We started the evening going into a couple of these. In one I discovered a taste for ginger beer. It was delicious, probably because it was served from stone jars. Then we found the place that was to become our local, The Setting Sun.

The main bar was like the sitting room of a house, with long tables and benches across the bay windows and the opposite wall, with a seat fixed to the wall behind the door. The small bar had just enough room for one person serving. There was a hatch at one side where people would bring jugs and bottles to be filled to take home. Anyone who wanted to use the room opposite would go into the corridor and collect their beer from there, as the old landlord rarely left the bar for long. He was too busy most of the night giving orders to his customers to be careful or be quiet. Not, I may add, to the youngsters, but to the old regulars who were real characters.

For instance there was the one who, after a good few drinks, attempted to do a very poor impression of a tap dance on top of the table. He seemed to have a liking for London. Whenever he saw Julie (one of the London girls) come into the bar, he would grab her hand and while she stood beside him, sing, "I wheeled her in me barrer, wheeled her up and down – she was the fairest of them all, the pride of London Town." Every now and then during the evening, through all the chatter, a loud burst of song came through from that direction. While elsewhere a voice shouted, "When I was a Sergeant Major at the Somme ..." to cries of, "Oh no, not again," as he tried to relate stories of his experiences in the First World War while his companion was up at the bar saying, "I'll just have one more half for the road". This performance was repeated throughout the evening until closing time.

Last but not least was the local cattle drover, a very large man who socially was a really nice person to talk to, but when working turned into a tough, brusque man who knew his job well. On market days he would drive the cattle (as many as 200 at a time) from the town through the main street, down to the railway station letting nothing and no one get in his way. Many a lone car driver fell victim to his wrath more than once.

If he saw a car approaching the herd he would point his walking stick and say, "Wait". Should the car try to move an inch he would charge through, waving the stick, issuing threats while the erring motorist cowered in his seat. To add further to his misery, the steers trying to get by would lift their tails and leave a deposit somewhere on the car, all to the delight of the young lads who would turn up on every market day to help with the cattle drive.

The fun continued for them as one steer panicked and crashed through the passage of a pub, only to find itself solidly jammed halfway into the toilet, the horns scraping away half the paintwork and wallpaper. Everyone stood around giving advice. At last someone climbed over the steer's back, pushing from his front end while the rest tugged with ropes from the back, leaving the toilet somewhat the worse for wear. Meanwhile the lads were trying to control the other steers but two dozen of them had already scattered over the open common. It took days to round them up to be put in a field until the cattle train came the next week.

As one irate lady came out to her doorstep and saw the mess that the herd had left inside the porch, she yelled, "What are you going to do about this?" The drover, still hustling on, turned around and said "Tell you what missis, if it isn't claimed in two weeks time you can keep it." Most people in the street ran to close every possible door and gate when they heard him coming. It was just hard luck if he got there first. I leave to the imagination the dilemma of the street when he was driving 200 sheep through.

The old iron stove in the middle of the pub bar had a pipe going up through the ceiling. This was so well stacked with fuel that at times it turned red with the heat. Many times an unwary person would get carried away talking on their favourite subject and place a drink on it. The glass would shatter, a cloud of steam rising as the beer cascaded over the hot plate, giving the already harassed landlord cause to shout, "Keep the glasses off the stove." It was a miracle the place was cleared at the ten-thirty closing time. Perhaps this was helped by the fact that most of us would be making our way to the dance.

This event appeared to be attended by every able person in the town, including people from the outlying farms and villages. The three piece band consisted of drums and cymbals, an accordion and a well used piano which was played with great enthusiasm. There were very few tunes they couldn't play, and the new songs coming out would be added each week. The three musicians showed they loved playing and singing as much as we all enjoyed dancing to their music. There was no lack of partners as the farmhands made the dance the highlight of their week.

As we neared the hostel, there was a loud clanging. Everyone started to hurry. The warden was leaning out of the kitchen window banging a frying pan with a soup ladle, warning us we had five minutes to get inside. The punishment for arriving back late was washing up after the evening meal for a week, and losing our late pass for the following Saturday night.

What struck me most about the people of Devon was the way we were all referred to as 'Maid'. For example, on meeting a farmer, he would say, "Come this way maid, I'll show you what's to be done". Although they asked what your name was, it was rarely used.

The farm lads, when in a gang together, always seemed to be bent on mischief. When we arrived at a farm and saw them sitting together nudging each other with wide grins on their faces, you could imagine them saying, "We'll have a bit of fun with these maids", little realising all the same tricks had been tried before.

One of their favourites was to wait until you turned your back to unpick a rick, and a sheaf would be hurled at you, sometimes knocking you off balance. Sometimes a new born baby mouse from a nest (there were many of these) was dropped down your back. The lads were very abashed when you calmly untucked your shirt to drop the creature back onto the rick. But it was all in good fun and they seemed to respect the fact that we were capable of working just as hard as they did.

On occasion, a girl was required for a week or two for general farm work. This was nice as you were treated as one of the family, going in for breakfast as you arrived each day and a full meal at dinner break. This time though there was an added bonus for me, a chance to fulfil an ambition I'd had for some time – learning to drive a tractor. This turned out to be quite simple. It was started by a handle and once it was merrily chugging away, you turned the petrol tap over onto 'tvc' and the fuel ran the engine all day. The difficult part was controlling the many different attachments used behind it, and also learning the art of backing trailers into gateways and outhouse buildings. But, with a bit of common sense, a lot of perseverance and patience on the part of the farmer, it could be done. Once this skill was learned, should a tractor driver be required for field work, you were sent there.

An old Fordson I had to start each morning was a real beast and constantly refused to start. It would give a little cough and then fade out. The starting handle would kick back at you with the strength of a horse's hoof, and this is why you were taught to place your thumb in line with the fingers over the handle. Should you grasp it in the normal way, you could end up with a badly damaged hand and wrist.

Approaching this monster ready for battle, I could almost imagine it chuckling in delight. After about ten minutes I would lost my cool, calling it names, giving it a hefty kick in the tyre all to no avail. One morning I thought perhaps a little coaxing may help; down on my knees with hands together I said, "Please start". After two or three turns it did just that, it was so ridiculous I could hardly climb into the seat, I was laughing so much.

The WAEC (War Agricultural Executive Committee) went on long after hostilities had ended, and employed many civilians who were not farmers but had knowledge of the land. They had taken over large stretches of moorland in the area, turning it into potato, sugar beet, mangold and corn fields.

Threshing was carried out there, the root crops were piled up into long caves covered with straw and earth until sorting time. A nearby farm was given the contract to provide the girls with hot drinks. Going down the farm lane to collect our drinks we would often find eggs in the hedges from the free running chickens. Washing an old tin out with tea we would light a small fire and cook them. Most times they ended up scrambled, but enjoyable. Walking beside the hedge on the way back to get the lorry, any more eggs we found were eaten raw from the shell. This would be frowned upon these days, but it never seemed to do us any harm.

At one farm I went to, I was warned beforehand that the farmer was a very rough mannered man who had a reputation for giving his wife and children a really hard time. He hardly spoke when I got there, except to tell me what to do and that I should "get on with it." Later in the day he drove up in a horse and cart. After we had finished loading this he told me to lead the horse on. Holding the halter, I clicked my teeth, as most people do, to make him move. The farmer immediately drew the animal to a halt, yelling at me, "Don't click at my horse like that, you speak to him in a proper manner." Covered in embarrassment I did as he said, but I was amazed that a man who treated human beings as he did should have such concern for a horse.

A local farm we really liked working at employed the Land Army most of the year. It was owned by an old retired farmer but was managed by his two sons. At potato sorting time the old man would join us in the barn and regale us with stories of his days as a youth, how he and his farmworker friends would rush to do their chores as quickly as possible, as they were promised that, should they finish in good time, they would be given sixpence and a lift in the horse and cart to the visiting fair ground in the town. We listened to him for hours with great interest, which made the day go by very swiftly.

Each morning we would go into the shippen and drink the warm milk from that morning's milking. As it was a Jersey herd, the milk was rich and sweet. We were always taken into the farm kitchen at meal times to share the family's food. On cold days we sat around the large black range used for cooking, an old iron kettle always hanging from the hook over the fire. There was incessant singing from crickets that lived in the chimney wall behind the stove; the old man said the kitchen would be a very lonely place without them, they had been there as long as he could remember.

I think farming in those days was harder but less stressful than now, things were much more natural. For instance, we would think nothing of drinking from a spring in a field, the water clear as crystal, cool and refreshing. One day we found watercress growing beside a small stream, picked it and put it in our sandwiches with no thought or worry about it being contaminated. The countryside in those days was a joy to be in – what a pity it had to change.

A couple of us were sent to work at the Annery, helping with the gardens. This was a very large old manor house set on a hill and could be clearly seen from the main road. As it was empty when we went there we decided to explore inside. The kitchen still had the large dressers, and looking in the drawers we found old newspapers used for lining. In the hall was a lovely polished wood staircase and a large room with beautiful dark blue silk paper on the walls. We could imagine how it must have been when it was filled with people; the servants and the gentry they worked for. It seemed unbelievable that no one lived there any more. It is very sad that a couple of years after we were there, this lovely old house was completely gutted by fire.

The threshing machines in Devon were an older version of those in Leamington, but to my mind they were better. Whereas the new machine had a flat top with a large opening for the drum, the older one here felt more secure as there was a box around the drum and a much narrower opening. It was slower as you had to be sure to cut each band and shake the sheaves more openly to avoid jamming, but it felt a great deal safer.

Barley was awful to work with as the sharp spines on the ears clung to your clothes and scratched the skin; it was best to brush your hair out in the open or they would be every-where. Many nights we spent hours picking the spines from our jumpers one by one. Lots of thistles grew among dredge corn (a mixture of barley and oats), and although they turned brown and shrivelled by threshing time, the spikes were still very sharp and would imbed themselves in your fingers as you lifted them to hold the band. It was a common sight to see girls armed with a pair of tweezers to pick them out.

Hot baths were really welcome to take the soreness from your skin. We were lucky to have an excellent maintenance man at this hostel who kept the boilers well fuelled giving us endless hot water, unlike some places where there had to be a rota for baths and the hot water ran out long before even this was covered. Although girls in from threshing were given priority, baths often had to be taken in lukewarm water.

On Tuesday nights we usually went the seven miles to Bideford to see a film. The lorry driver, a local man, always set aside this evening to take us. After the show he would collect us, travelling at full speed along the road before the chip shop closed. It was a small business, converted from a front room in a house, but the chips were so delicious I can never remember tasting others like them. The owner always said it was a special recipe known only to him. Although each night at the hostel a jug of cocoa and a tray of bread and dripping or bread and jam was left out for us, we still enjoyed our treat of chips after our night at the cinema.

Apart from this, we didn't make a habit of going out much in the week, except perhaps the ones with boyfriends or the occasional date. We would often lie on our bunks talking across to each other, or writing letters. With so many girls in one large area, there was always something to discuss of interest. Funnily enough, although we talked of our families, you rarely heard anyone say they were homesick, or complain of boredom. Everyone seemed quite content with what they were doing. Of course there were a few grumbles about small things, but nothing to really worry about. Considering the hours spent together both at work and socially, it was surprising that arguments were rare. Should a difference of opinion arise it was soon sorted out and forgotten.

Looking at the work rota, we were puzzled to see a gang of us were booked to go to Torrington railway station. We wondered what kind of job we could be needed for, but on arrival we soon found out. There were truck loads of field drainage pipes waiting to be transferred to lorries taking them to work sites and so we formed a chain, throwing the pipes from one to another. It was hard work, but enjoyable. The trouble was, no one had warned us to take gloves with us, the result being that by lunch break the rough clay edges of the pipes had skinned our hands. We decided to take our socks off and use them for protection, but by the end of the day even they were a bit worse for wear. I must say a Land Girl's hands were the least of her feminine charms, always covered in hard callouses and broken nails, but there was little we could do about it.

Who your work partner was made a great difference to the day, especially when potato picking. I always found it quite difficult to work with one particular girl as after we had picked up a couple of rows, and the weather was a little cold, her fingers would go white and numb so she would sit on the sack of potatoes massaging her hands whilst I struggled to do her work for her. I'm sure she would have been better moving about, but team work was so good that the rest of the girls would take a longer patch each, leaving me with a little less to do.

It was the night of the fancy dress dance and we had been working for weeks on different ideas. At last I decided to dress up as Old Mother Riley, an outlandish old film character, and Babs was to be her daughter Kitty, who on screen was her mother's pride and joy. My costume was a large woollen shawl held together by an enormous safety pin, an old battered hat with a flower in front (a Land Army hat cut in half) and tied with a wide ribbon, a tattered ankle-length skirt and a pair of rubber boots with laces. Babs' dress was a crinoline made from crepe paper held out by hoops of wire, a pretty blouse and lots of make up. My cheeks were bright red with rouge and bright red lipstick. In the films she was a heavy drinker, and so I carried an empty bottle of whisky.

The crowd in the hall stared when we walked in, but really showed their appreciation as we walked around for the judging by clapping and shouting for Old Mother Riley. We came second. The winner was nicely dressed in a Queen Elizabeth I costume. We didn't mind not winning at all, we had only entered for the sheer fun of taking part. Despite my big clumsy boots and ragged appearance, I had plenty of partners asking me to dance. Most of them admired my daring to dress like that.

Babs' crinoline skirt came to grief as the hoops slipped down, but she stepped out of them and carried on regardless. We had a great time; it had been well worth all the planning.

The time seemed to have flown by since coming to Torrington; we were now in December. Babs had a steady boyfriend, but we remained the best of friends.

Threshing was still in full swing, as was ditching and pulling root crops. We walked to nearby farms. There were no bikes here; they would have been pretty useless for every mile you cycled you would have had to push it up hill for the next two.

Some days when we were rained off we stayed in the hostel, but mostly we were taken to an old camp at Handy Cross in Bideford where we sat in a Nissen hut darning holes in old potato sacks with a large bag needle threaded with string. These we stacked in their hundreds. The sacks belonged to seed merchants who used them time and time again once they had been repaired. Some joker looked in and suggested we paint arrows on our overalls to look the part for this job.

We also worked for the same merchants tipping out sackfuls of seed potatoes, breaking off all the old growing shoots, re-bagging and weighing up the now clean potatoes for sale. Some of them were so overgrown they were welded together and we had to jump on the sacks to break them apart before we could get them out of the bag. I suppose thinking about this, it could have been called saving work for a rainy day.

Christmas was nearly upon us again, and after yet another hilarious night in the Setting Sun, we were packed and ready for home. We boarded the train at Torrington, getting off again at Barnstaple, changing to the mainline train for Exeter. I was the last one to climb in and, slamming the train door behind me, I trapped my thumb in the hinged part of the door. Someone rushed to re-open it and, feeling very sick and faint, I looked at the damage. My nail had been crushed into tiny pieces while the flesh part was split open.

We tried to get help while waiting for a connection at Exeter, but it was late evening and no one knew where I could get first aid. The journey from there was a sheer nightmare, the constant throbbing almost unbearable. As we neared Gloucester, a sailor came into our carriage and asked what was wrong, and immediately took out a handkerchief and tied it tightly around my wrist. After a while the throbbing eased a little. I gave him my grateful thanks as he got off the train.

Babs and I stretched out on the seats of the now empty carriage and fell into an exhausted sleep. When we awoke we found to our dismay we had travelled on to a small station an hour's ride outside Birmingham. It was now early morning and we were told the only train that would be stopping there now was the milk train at 7am. All we could do was wait.

Arriving back in the city we found an emergency chemist open. They were most sympathetic and very concerned that I had been travelling like this for 13 hours. They cleaned and dressed my thumb, put my arm in a sling and gave me painkillers. They were so kind and helpful, it felt good to be attended to at last.

Babs' house was much nearer than mine so I went home with her. We slept the whole day and well into the evening so I was more than refreshed to travel home across Birmingham to start my leave on Christmas Eve.

During the holiday I redressed my injury every day, and although it was still very sore, it was healing slowly. I really enjoyed my leave and had lots of time to explain to my step-mother and sister all about where I now lived. We had a much longer leave than in Leamington due to the extended time allowed for travelling plus the fact we were too far away to go home on short weekend leave.

We returned the evening before New Year's Eve. I reported my injury to the warden who put me on light hostel duties for a week. The hand I had damaged was the right one, and being left handed I was not so handicapped as I might otherwise have been.

New Year's Eve was great fun. We toured the town pubs, the Setting Sun regulars were in great form, the war stories coming thick and fast, the singing louder than ever owing to an over-indulgence of their favourite brew. Even our dancer found it impossible to reach his table top stage, so settled for a slight shuffle where he stood. The cattle drover had driven his herd to the station for the hundredth time that evening. The landlord had given up trying to keep order; with a resigned look on his face he refilled their glasses and said nothing.

The dance was crowded, with everyone really enjoying themselves. The band was in full swing and we danced until nearly midnight, when everyone in the hall raced for the door and across the town square where we followed a tradition which had seen in every New Year for many years – linking hands around the Christmas tree to the strains of Old Lang Syne. 1948 had arrived.

CHAPTER FIVE

I cannot say I enjoyed my week of light duties. It seemed strange to watch the girls go off to work each day leaving the hostel so quiet. I felt very lost and left out of things, so it was with a sense of relief that I climbed into the lorry to get back to real work.

We were in a field next to the farmhouse clearing docks, digging each one individually with a weeding tool. After our lunch break we told Mary it was her turn to take the tea tray back to the farmhouse. Mary was not very happy about this as, although her rosy complexion made her look like a country girl, she was in fact a city girl who had not yet overcome her nervousness of farm animals. We all watched as Mary picked her way through the thick mire in the yard and then, as she came back, we all started to shout, "Quick Mary, the bull's out". She panicked, started to run, and fell face down into the thick of it. We went to help her up, covered in muck from top to toe, and sent her back into the farmhouse to clean up.

When Mary came out, we all stared in disbelief. She was a tiny 5ft 2in girl, and the farmer's wife, whose clothes she was wearing, was about three times her size. Huge overalls tied in with a thick leather belt made her look like a balloon ready for take off. We literally fell about laughing. She was rather cross with us for a little while, but then saw the funny side and laughed with us, vowing to get us back one day.

In the Setting Sun one evening, I met John, home on leave from Germany where he was stationed with the Army. I had seen him on several occasions and thought he looked rather nice and quite good looking. He didn't show much interest in girls and so I was most surprised when he asked if I would meet him next day – his nineteenth birthday. I discovered later it was Babs who had persuaded him to do this, and it had taken him quite a while to approach me as he was extremely shy.

As there was little to do on Sundays we went for a long walk, which was a good way of really getting to know each other. He told me he had two weeks of his leave left before returning to Germany and asked if I would meet him the next evening, which I did, and continued to do so each night for the rest of his leave. We promised to write to each other while he was away, and meet again when his leave came around in three months time.

I missed my evenings out after he had gone back, but still had plenty of things to amuse me in the hostel, especially one night a couple of weeks later.

It was quiet, and everyone had settled down for the night when someone said in a loud whisper, "Did you hear that?" We all listened. Sure enough there was someone creeping around outside. Panic ensued. "It's a prowler, quick fetch the warden," someone screamed. Grabbing anything we could to defend ourselves with, we waited.

The warden bustled in, hair piled up with curlers. Opening the window she shouted in her most commanding, official voice, "I know you are out there. Show yourself. The police are coming so give yourself up." No reply. "Right, girls," she said, "let's go get 'em."

Hanging on to each other, we filed out of the door using the warden's large frame as a shield while she waved a large walking stick in the air, shouting "Tally ho!" We found the intruder – a cow who had inadvertently wandered into the garden and was happily munching away at the cabbages we had planted.

After we had recovered from the shock, there was a great deal of merriment, especially when someone remarked, "If there had been a bloke out there he would either have been trampled into the ground or beaten the record for the four minute mile."

We finally settled back into our beds and were quiet once more, except for the occasional chuckle from different bunks as we thought about the night's events.

Many stories came in from the farms each night, and were a great source of amusement at the meal tables. Jean, like the rest of us, found it hard at first to understand the Devonshire dialect, and was helping the farmer to load a trailer when he called out, "Pass me that sack will 'ee." Puzzled, she looked around, then carried on working. The farmer repeated his request again, and then shouted, "Be you deaf maid, why don't 'ee answer me?" Jean replied, "Oh, were you talking to me? I was wondering who the heck Willie was."

Rosie had a somewhat stinging experience hoeing plants in a field when a low flying plane suddenly appeared. Thinking it was going to crash land, she panicked and ran at full speed, not looking where she was going, and landed face first into a hedge full of nettles.

Thelma, Pat and a few others were not very happy planting potatoes on a large estate, and came in each night with badly aching backs. As a rule when planting potatoes you paced out the distance where each one was to be placed. They were then planted by just stooping slightly and dropping it in the row. On this occasion however, the manager insisted that each potato was placed firmly in the ground. It must have been very difficult as they had to carry the heavy basket at the same time. I don't suppose they grew any better than other farm crops, but it was a case of doing whatever you were told to do, the way you were told to do it.

I was cleaning out a shippen and for some reason one cow was left behind. I was in a great mood, singing at the top of my voice, brooming down the messy gutters into a drainage hole in the wall. The cow stayed lying down and refused to budge so I said, "Right, that's it, your tail's in my way – down the drain it goes," and carried on brushing. She heaved herself up, at the same time swishing her tail full of mess, which whipped itself right across my face. Washing it off at the tap outside, I smiled to myself as the thought came to me that it would have been pretty useless to have tried to explain to her I was only joking!

Jean was sent to help out a farmer who had a broken leg, and she was to take over his job delivering milk in a pony and trap to the houses of a small village. On finishing this task, he told her it was essential that the boar was let out that day to serve the sows. This seemed simple enough, until the boar decided he was more interested in chasing her. When she saw him closing in for the attack she scrambled up the nearest bank – with great difficulty, as it was covered in thick slime and mud, and she was sliding down faster than she could climb up. She finally managed to reach the top and found there was no way down and so had to walk nearly a mile along the hedge until she found a place to get back down onto the road. On seeing this mud-soaked figure descending down the hedge, the people in the cottages opposite asked if she was alright. She answered that she was, but the boar would be in a heap of trouble when she got back!

Very often our dinner breaks turned into fun-time, as was the case when we were trimming hedges. To do this we used a stick to hold back any thorny growth, while cutting away the branches with a hook. This day we decided to play at being very dumb new army recruits being drilled by an irate sergeant. Using our sticks as rifles, we stood at ease in a very disorderly fashion, slumped over and standing at angles from the sublime to the ridiculous. Being called to attention and right turn, we moved in every direction, and when told to march, half went one way and half the other and we carried on walking when told to halt. The rifle drill was something to behold, with sticks flying everywhere. The sergeant's stern attitude was slowly breaking down. We were forced to stop as some of us were suffering stomach cramps from laughing so much, while others were bordering on hysteria. It would seem unbelievable after all this that a short while later we were back seriously concentrating on the task of hedging, but we did just that.

Pat was ironing a piece of cloth which she had dyed bright red to wear as a turban to cover her hair the next day. This was a triangle, usually bought from the chemist as an arm sling, most of us used these as it was more economical then buying scarves. While doing this she told us of an incident that happened on a nearby farm. On this particular day Pat had been sent out to work alone, except for three Italian prisoners of war who spoke no English. It was a very hot day and, turning round, she saw the men about to take off their trousers. Covered in embarrassment she ran off the field and told the farmer. He went off to investigate and came back laughing, telling her it was alright, they had shorts on underneath. "Well," she said, "I'm still not going back there. I shall feel a right fool now," and made her way back to the hostel. She had to put up with a lot of teasing from the farmer whenever she was working there, as she often did.

Although the war ended in 1945, the Italian and German prisoners of war were still in this country in 1947. I had worked with many in Leamington and related that same evening to Pat how pleasant and courteous they had been to work with. They would often show us the things they were making in the camp to pass away the time. One man had made a ship in a bottle for his mother, while others had carved wooden toys to give to their children when they finally got home.

One giant of a man insisted on lifting heavy sacks for us, saying they were too much for us to manage. Normally we didn't expect help like this as it was part of our work to lift one hundredweight sacks of potatoes from the ground to a trailer without giving it a second thought.

We sat with the POWs at meal breaks while they tried to teach us a few words of the German language. I recalled how concerned they were one day when a farmer brought them out a hot meal while we were left with just our sandwiches. They could not understand why they were the ones to get the best treatment. We told them not to worry, just to eat the meal and enjoy it, but somehow I don't think they did.

We did encounter one man who still seemed very bitter, and would stand apart from us all, giving us an icy stare when we looked his way. He never attempted to speak, not even to his companions. It seemed he was still having his own private war, so we just had to leave him to it.

We felt a great deal of pity for them when they talked with such sadness of the longing to see their families again. It had been a long time and they must have felt worlds apart from them all.

No one could say we didn't try to put some variety into the town, especially when we invited the men from the dairy to form a football team and challenged them to play a match against us; although we only knew a little about the game, we were determined to have a go. They duly agreed to play on a Saturday evening in April at the local football ground.

The match was well supported by the townsfolk who cheered us on as we went onto the field dressed in shirts, our working boots and an assortment of shorts cut down from old dungarees and breeches. We were ready for the off, and threw ourselves into the game with great enthusiasm, especially Peggy the goalkeeper, leaping in all directions and making saves that would have put a world cup goalie to shame.

The referee was an ex-footballer so knew all the rules but seemed to be on our side, helping us all the way. We were awarded several penalties and it seemed all the fouls were given against the men. Not quite fair really, as the score proved: Land Army 8, Workers 2, thanks to the ref and goal-keeper, but taking nothing away from the way we really tried to put our all into the match. It had been great fun, and both teams joined in a celebration drink together afterwards. Although we were very fit and used to exercise, next morning found us almost unable to walk, our leg muscles seized up and groaning "never again".

Saturday 24th April was the day Anne was to be married to a local lad. We were very excited about this, although I felt I would miss her as we had had lots of fun and spent many hours together in the communal lounge with the radio playing full blast while we practised new Jive routines to try out at the dance each week.

We had promised to do our utmost to get to the church in time for the ceremony, so it was chaos at the hostel when we jumped from the lorries, rushing to change from our working clothes and dash into town. We just made it.

Anne looked really lovely in her wedding dress, and was most surprised and pleased when she saw two lines of girls in full uniform outside the church door holding pitchforks tied with white ribbons, forming an arch for the bride and groom to walk through. We were delighted to have been in time to do this for her. It had been a closely guarded secret for some time.

Our pleasure soon turned to dismay on arriving back at the hostel, as all our clothes and personal belongings had been thrown into one big heap in the passage outside the sleeping quarters. We were extremely angry and confronted the warden about this. She told us it had been done to teach us a lesson not to leave anything lying around in future. We did know the rule – that everything always had to be put away after use – and we always kept to it, but, knowing the special circumstances and the time factor, it seemed to us most unfair, and so out of character, for her to do a thing like this, especially that she had chosen this one day to spoil it all. The punishment did not end there. We were banned from going to a special celebration party that night.

The evening meal was boycotted by us all that night, and we told the warden that no one would be turning out for work until our protest was heard by an official. So, an urgent phone message was sent by the warden to the private home of one of the officials.

A few of us were determined to go to the party. We waited until about 9.30 when all was quiet. We climbed out of the lounge window, which was then closed by one of the other girls when we had gone, and although we were rather nervous about going against orders, we managed to enjoy the night while the girls inside the hostel stayed awake to open the windows for us on our return.

Early Monday morning found the official from Exeter HQ on the doorstep. After talking to us she admitted we had some cause for complaint, but told us she thought it would be better to accept what had happened, put it all behind us and get the hostel back to its normal happy atmosphere. The warden admitted she had acted a little hastily, and so we went to work later that same morning, deciding to do as the official asked. We hadn't really enjoyed being so rebellious, but for once our good humoured approach to life had been very sorely tried.

The May Fair celebration on the first Thursday in May was a wonderful time, something we had never seen before. Although we were working on the actual day, we went to the dance a few nights before to see the carnival queen and her attendants be picked from the local girls. We also went into town on the Wednesday evening to watch the school children rehearse dancing around the Maypole and crowning their May queen, getting ready for the real thing next day.

A few weeks before all this we had agreed to enter in the carnival. In those days all the lorries were provided by the dairy, and the driver would hurry to do his rounds in the morning to enable us to decorate it in the afternoon, then give his services to drive around in the carnival that evening. Only about ten girls could ride, but everyone joined in the preparation beforehand. Each one wore a crepe paper costume depicting a different vegetable – cabbage, carrot, potato and so on. Only the girls' faces were visible, with sheaves stacked in place, paper flowers all around the chains outside, it was really wonderful. We were pleased to come second in our category.

We decided to give the prize money to the cottage hospital, and this was announced over the loud speakers (the last thing we expected). The crowd showed their appreciation at the gesture, and it left us more popular than ever with the local people.

Babs had parted company with her boyfriend and appeared to be rather unsettled, so I was not too surprised when she said she was leaving for good. I was very sad to be losing such a good friend, but I knew she would be unhappy if she stayed.

Accompanying her to the railway station, we said our goodbyes and I promised to write and pay her a visit when home on leave. As I watched the train until it was out of sight, I remembered how, as new arrivals, we had laughed at being at the end of the line. It seemed as though that was just what this day was for Babs.

Back at the hostel I was feeling a little forlorn as I sat on my bunk in the empty cubicle. The other two girls who had been there had been given transfers to other places. Peggy called to me from further down the hut and suggested I might as well pick up my belongings and move into the empty bunk with her and two other girls sharing the cubicle. I appreciated this thoughtful gesture and accepted.

I was delighted when one of the girls asked me to go horse riding with her one Sunday morning. This was Flo, who had an absolute mania for horses. She would cut out pictures of horses from magazines with the same fervour the rest of us had for our favourite film stars. Evidently she had found a farmer who owned gymkhana horses and was looking for someone to exercise them. Flo needed no persuasion. I found myself really looking forward to it, even though I was probably the worst recruit for the job as all I had managed up to now was ambling along on a cart-horse.

Deciding to take the horses on the open common, we followed an upward path. She told me to urge my mount into a trot. Finding I was enjoying this, I decided to go a little faster and broke into a canter. The end of the path was obscured by a bend. I heard Flo calling and, glancing behind me I saw her waving and so I waved back, shouting, "I'm OK, it's really great." Fortunately the horse slowed down at the bend, and we just managed to stop before we reached a large gate. Flo arrived very ashen faced, and yelled, "Didn't you hear me? I was trying to tell you the gate was there. You could have hurt him." I felt a little rebuffed that she was only worried about the horse, but I suppose in a way she was right, especially for someone who thought these animals were the most important things in life.

Flo often went out on her boyfriend's motorbike. One evening he arrived accompanied by a friend, and Flo asked if I would like to go out with them. It was great riding around the country lanes. I learned that my companion, Pete, was a farmer's son and also that he had a great sense of humour. After that night we often went out on the bikes at weekends, ending up at the Saturday dance.

It was made quite clear to him at the beginning that I was writing to John, and intended to see him when he came home. Pete settled for this, which made our outings easy going and enjoyable, but they soon ended when a farmer offered Flo and myself two spaniel puppies. We really wanted them, but wondered if we could persuade the warden to let us keep them.

We came up with a plan to try and prove to her it could be possible. We acquired two large wooden barrels and placed them in the small field behind the hostel and drove two tying stakes into the ground, attaching long chains to these. When everything was prepared we went to find the warden. We took her to show her what we had done and pleaded with her to let us have the puppies. She hesitated at first and explained to us she was afraid that everyone would want to bring dogs home. So we had to make sure the other girls would have no objection to us having them. Knowing no more dogs would be allowed they readily agreed, and even offered to help us look after our two.

We couldn't wait to bring them home. Flo chose the very boisterous pure black pup and called her Beauty. I chose the smallest of the litter. He was black and white and sat quietly apart from the others, but ran to me when I called him. I decided he would be Timmy.

It was lovely to get home from work each day to see how they greeted us, tails wagging, jumping around in excitement. We had bought them two large bowls each for food and water. There was never any shortage of things to eat, collected from the kitchen. We spent all our spare time grooming them until their coats shone, teaching them to fetch the sticks we threw for them, and generally chasing around the field.

Beauty was growing faster than Timmy, and after a while I realised all was not well with him. As I was tending him one day I noticed he appeared to be having a slight fit. I asked the vet to have a look at him and he prescribed some medication and said Timmy would be alright as long as he was not over-tired or excited too much.

The author, working in a field.

Tibs, Jean and Ginger, three of the author's friends from Leamington Spa, the first posting. They all met on the train on their very first day and were to remain good friends.

Outside Flo's home in Liverpool. The author is on the right.

Right: Flo's sister and the author on Merseyside

Lily and Joyce, Land Army girls, at Bromson Hill Hostel, Warwickshire. c. 1946

At the Torquay Convalescent Home. The author is 3rd from right, back row.

Left: Sheila (Babs) Goodison, the author's friend, in the doorway of the Torrington Hostel

Torrington, April 1948. The Land Army girls challenged the men from the dairy to a football match. The girls are in an improvised kit of working boots, breeches and shorts cut down from dungarees. Final score: Land Army 8, Dairy Workers 2.

*Torrington,
April 1948.
The Land Army
football team
which beat the
Dairy Workers.
The author is
kneeling on the
right*

Saturday 24th April 1948, Anne's wedding.
Having rushed to change into uniform after work, the girls just made it in time to form a guard of honour outside the church, using their decorated pitchforks as an arch.

The Land Army's entry in the 1948 Torrington Carnival as part of the May Fair celebrations. They earned second place and donated the prize money to Torrington Cottage Hospital, where, on leaving the Land Army in 1950, the author returned to nursing.

Left: The author on one of the horses she and Flo exercised for a local farmer.

Right: Beauty and Timmy, the two spaniels Flo and the author kept while living at the Torrington hostel.

The Bromson Hill House Hostel, Lighthorne, Warwickshire, 1947 ...

... and as it is today in 2004

A Land Army Girl
On joining the WLA, every girl was supplied with the following: 2 green jerseys,
2 pairs of breeches, 2 overall coats, 2 pairs of dungarees, 6 pairs of stockings, 3 shirts,
1 pair of ankle boots, 1 pair of shoes, 1 pair of gumboots or boots with leggings, 1 hat,
1 overcoat with shoulder titles, 1 oilskin or mackintosh, 2 towels, an oilskin sou'-wester,
a green armlet, and a metal badge.

Land Army girls were employed in all manner of general farmwork

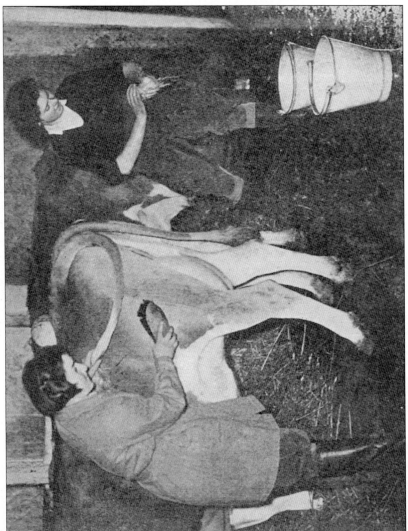

Milking and Dairy Work were important duties for the Land Army

Feeding Calves

Hoeing

Being allowed to plough a field on their own for the first time was a proud moment for any Land Army girl

Threshing

Land Army work was very physically demanding

Leading cows to and from the field – part of the daily routine for the Land Army girls.

Land Army girls were expected to tend a flock of sheep; including lambing, dipping and shearing

Sorting potatoes – a tedious, yet necessary job

Ditching

BACK TO THE LAND

Words by
P. ADKINS, W.L.A. 28299 & J. MONCRIEFF

Music by
E. K. LORING, W.L.A. 2053

1

Back to the Land, we must all lend a hand,
To the farms and the fields we must go.
There's a job to be done,
Though we can't fire a gun
We can still do our bit with the hoe.
When your muscles are strong
You will soon get along,
And you'll think that a country life's grand.
We're all needed now,
We must all speed the plough,
So come with us—Back to the Land.

2

Back to the Land, with its clay and its sand,
Its granite and gravel and grit,
You grow barley and wheat
And potatoes to eat
To make sure that the nation keeps fit.
Remember the rest
Are all doing their best,
To achieve the results they have planned
We will tell you once more
You can help win the war
If you come with us—Back to the Land.

Single copies 1d. each, 2d. post free, or 12 for 1s., post free, can be obtained from the Editor, " The Land Girl," Balcombe Place, Balcombe, Hayward's Heath, Sussex

The warden and kitchen staff were marvellous, keeping an eye on him when I was not there, and he showed no sign of getting worse. So I just gave him lots of loving care. He was quite happy and he did have Beauty for company.

It was nearing time for John to come home on leave. We had been writing to each other regularly and I was looking forward to seeing him again, so was most disappointed to receive a letter to say he would not be arriving after all because all leave had been cancelled owing to the Berlin air lift (a dispute between the Russians and other occupying forces over there), so it could be months before he would be home again. So I decided to go home on leave myself as this was long overdue.

Starting to make arrangements for my journey, Flo came to me and suggested she took her leave at the same time and we could spend half of our leave at my home in Birmingham, going for the rest of the time up to Liverpool to stay with her mother. This seemed a good arrangement, and would be a really nice break.

My stepmother and sister were most interested to hear all about Devon, and I told them I would try and find somewhere for them to stay when I got back, and they must come down on holiday. We all went out together shopping in the city, and visited several places to meet friends and relations. It was very enjoyable, as it was in Liverpool where we took trips on the boat across the Mersey and visited the fairgrounds, finding time also to go horseback riding on the beach. It had been a nice arrangement which we repeated on many other home leaves.

CHAPTER SIX

I t came as a great blow to us all when, out of the blue, we were told that we were all to be split up and transferred to different hostels as the Torrington Hostel was going to be used to house displaced persons from Poland who would then take over our jobs on the farms.

This news was greeted with some trepidation by the farmers as they had by now been used to having the girls working for them for a long time. They knew we had the experience to do the work and now they would have to start training these men who possibly knew nothing about farming, plus there was the disadvantage of the language barrier. Once again we had to comply with the orders from the WAEC but were very unhappy to do so.

One dilemma was what to do with the dogs as we certainly would not be allowed to take them with us until we knew where we would be living. Flo asked her boyfriend to take

Beauty, while Pete offered to take Timmy to his farm. We knew they would be well looked after, so had to be content with that arrangement for the time being.

Finally the dreaded day arrived. We drove through the town in the back of the lorry, all of us crying quite openly. There was no cheerful singing that day. The townsfolk who saw us drive by waved and wished us luck, but this only seemed to make us feel sadder than ever.

We dropped several girls off at the Instow Hostel, a large house on the sea front. Brenda, Evelyn, Flo, Eva and myself then went on to Barnstaple where we found a large three storey house situated in the main street of the town. Our new home.

We were taken to a small room on the third floor, again bunk beds and lockers were the only furniture there. Four of us were given this room while Eva was taken to another room to share with others. The recreation room on the ground floor overlooked the main street through large bay windows. A large fireplace had a log fire burning in it and looked quite homely. A piano stood against the wall, and I thought it would be interesting to see if I could learn to play that some-time. While talking to the other girls when they came in from work, we found we would be working in a much larger area than Torrington. A lot of the farms were situated along the North Devon coastline.

It was to one of these I went first. The lorry was to take us to the gate where the farmer was waiting. We were hoeing that day. To do this you carefully thinned out the rows of plants to leave one single plant every few inches which allowed it plenty of room to grow to its full size. It had been known for a girl still new to the job to hoe out all the plants leaving only the weeds behind.

The field we were in this day seemed to be on very high ground. The farmer had told us earlier to start out in good time to fetch our tea from the farm as it was quite a long walk down. Two of us set out to do this. On rounding a bend in the lane we came to a complete standstill, the view in front of us was absolutely breathtaking. The whole panorama of Combe Martin Bay stretched out in front of us, the wide expanse of vivid blue sea in the harbour, the small fishing and pleasure boats bobbing about. The white cottages so picturesque with flowers adorning the walls and gardens. We immediately ran back to fetch the others, to show them what we had seen. It was sheer enchantment.

Flo couldn't believe her eyes while we were working together at another farm and looked across the fields and spied about a dozen pure Arabian horses grazing. Dinner break food forgotten, we sped across the fields to examine them closer. While standing in the centre of the field surrounded by these really magnificent creatures, they decided to take a closer look at the intruders and started to close in on us. Watching them do this suddenly felt rather menacing and we felt a sense of fear and hurriedly made our exit. We were a little shamefaced afterwards as they probably were just being inquisitive, but we thought it better to be safe than sorry.

Settling into life in the hostel was easy, the warden was extremely nice. One of the girls, Lesley, was a large robust person, very full of fun, and we got on well together. Going past her room one night, I made a jokey comment about her. She dragged me into the room and a wrestling match ensued with everyone cheering us on. Realising the odds were against me, with her twelve stone to my seven, speed was of the essence. I tore out of the room with Lesley in hot pursuit, managing to reach my room and lock the door before she caught up with me. It had been good fun, but enough was enough, at least it had given the others a good laugh.

Jose on the other hand was the exact opposite with little or no sense of humour.

Everyone loved tinkering on the piano. Whenever they started Jose would walk out saying she didn't like the din they were making, declaring how much she hated that piano. Coming in from the cinema one night, the girls went into the lounge to find her on her hands and knees trying to saw the loud pedal off the piano. Luckily they had been in time to stop her finishing off the job, so no real harm was done, but it was a great source of amusement and was a much eagerly related tale when any new girl asked why there was a deep cut in the piano pedal, also adding it was just Jose trying to put her point of view across.

However, although we had settled, Flo and I decided we would still spend our weekends in Torrington – getting the bus there on Saturday afternoon, and catching the last one back at ten thirty on Sunday night – so we were still able to attend the dances and mix with the locals there, also giving us the opportunity to see Timmy and Beauty.

We found a landlord of an old inn who gave us accommodation and provided us with meals. He and his wife were a really loveable old couple who treated us as their own. They charged us a ridiculously low fee for this, and we were free to come and go as we pleased. They seemed as happy to have us as we were to be there.

It was around this time I started having doubts about my relationship with John, although we were still writing regularly. I found myself being teased by his friends at dances when I danced with anyone, and they told me they would be giving John a report on all this when he came home. Although I knew it was all meant in good fun by them, it made me wonder if I was doing the right thing, as after all I had only known him for two weeks, and it was now five months since I had seen him, but I decided to wait a while longer before making my decision.

Privacy was the thing most sadly lacking in both the hostel and at work; in fact it was non-existent. For instance, you could be quietly minding your own business, having a long hot soak in the bath, only to hear someone calling you. Answering them, a head would appear over the top of the partition separating the bathrooms, and carry on a long conversation about something that just couldn't wait until you came out. On other occasions, for the want of something better to do, they would fire missiles of any sort over that same wall, and any thought of relaxing and having a few minutes to yourself was lost.

On the farms there were no toilet facilities whatsoever, you just found a hedge that was as far as possible out of sight of any men who were working with you. Mostly they took no notice of this, even when we were using machinery and our absence was obvious, but there was the inevitable one exception.

Working near the farm yard, we found the only hedge we could use had a house right at the other end of the field, but it was quite a decent distance away, so it seemed alright. Dinner break found us all lined along that same hedge before the men came back. During the afternoon one of them, with a sickly grin all over his face, shouted to the other, "I saw something real funny when I went home, a whole line of squatters along that hedge." Chuckling away he added, "course, I had to get the binoculars out first." He lived in the house across the field.

Normally we laughed embarrassing situations off, but in this case we felt he had gone out of his way to intrude into something that was difficult at the best of times, and told him so in no uncertain terms. Possibly this would have seemed a very funny situation to some, but not to us.

We certainly managed to cope with rough conditions, but still had a great deal of pride left to preserve.

One morning I was asked to take a new recruit with me to show her the ropes. We were working on the rather smelly job of creosoting the chicken houses. Walking up the farm lane we met the farmer, looking very agitated. He asked us to jump onto the trailer, explaining to us that dogs had attacked his sheep during the night.

The scene in front of us was devastating, dead ewes scattered everywhere. Some had run into the stream and were just lying there in the water. It was unfortunate that it had to happen to our new girl on her first day, as it was a most unpleasant task to lift them and fling them onto the trailer, especially when one of them made a loud noise as we did so. She screamed, "It's still alive," but it was only the gasses from its stomach. I could see her getting very weary and tearful, so I was glad when the job was finished.

Going back to the task we had started out to do, I did my best to get the conversation going in another direction, trying to make her laugh until she finally relaxed. I explained that most days were really good fun, that she had done the worst day's work first, and that it should be plain sailing for her after this.

Market gardening was much lighter than field work; mostly weeding, potting plants or picking tomatoes, peas and beans. The owner of the place Evelyn and I were sent one day lived alone in a bungalow. As there were only two of us, he asked us in for a tea break, apologising for the untidiness of the place, and said he had such little time to keep it as he would like, owing to the outside work taking up so much of his day.

After a discussion between us, Evelyn and I approached him rather hesitantly with the suggestion that if he could spare us from the outdoor work, we would be more than willing to spend a couple of hours giving the place a thorough going over, and also cook him a good meal. He seemed very pleased at the idea, but said if we were doing a meal for him, to cook enough for us to join him.

We found lamb chops in the fridge, and decided to make a roast dinner with peas and fresh mint. After preparing this we set about the cleaning, and worked with real commitment until everything was sparkling clean. We realised how hard it must be to try to run a smallholding and keep house alone. He was such a nice person, we felt rather sorry for him. We laid the table with care to make it look really nice, although we had little chance to cook and we had prepared the meal by trial and error, he ate it with great relish and we agreed it hadn't been too bad after all. He said it was good to see the house looking so nice and wished he was able to afford to employ us more often. For us it had been a really lovely day, and most rewarding to have given a hardworking, rather lonely man so much pleasure by just having a really good idea.

Moira was a natural comedienne and a joy to work with. On the gloomiest of days, her quick repartee in different situations kept us laughing most of the time. I had split the ankle part of one of my wellington boots and was dropping potatoes in the drills. Every time I placed my foot forward the boot gaped open. On noticing this, Moira said, "Oh look, Little

Chief Laughing Boot." Naturally, after this, each time I looked down I could see the split open up into a wide smile, and just couldn't stop laughing. In the end I just sat on a sack of potatoes until I could keep a straight face to be able to carry on working.

Moira and I worked together for many days, sorting potatoes in barns, and passed away the hours thinking how we could make a living when we were finished with the Land Army by starting our own private business.

Our first idea was to buy a mare, renting a couple of stables, getting her put in foal, and starting our own riding stable. We went into great detail working out the ups and downs of this project. The downs had it, as we said in the end, by the time it had even got off the ground we would probably have been in our dotage.

Idea number two seemed much more feasible. This was to rent a bit of ground, hammer together a few sheds, buy a good cockerel and a few hens and start a chicken farm. We agreed we had to start on a minute scale, even small would have been too big, as at this moment in time neither one of us had two halfpennies to rub together, but nevertheless we carried on regardless, we even got as far as naming it "The Chickery". Then came the crunch; it was alright with our field and sheds, but how about our own living quarters? We considered a tent, and that was as far as it went.

It had been good to have our dreams, no doubt we would have many more, none of them able to get further than our own imagination, but they certainly helped to pass away the time of what could have been a long, boring day.

Many small things gave us pleasure, such as the time we were working in a field alongside the railway line. I recall the two elderly sisters who were employing us at the time would bring out large mugs of really delicious coffee and showed so much pride when we told them how enjoyable this was.

The Devon Belle was a luxury coastal steam train mainly used for the holiday trade. Each day at the same time we would wait to see it appear in the distance, knowing that as soon as the driver saw us he would give out several loud blasts on the whistle, and both he and the fireman, and most of the holiday makers would wave until they were nearly out of sight.

It quite made our day as sometimes working in the fields made you feel quite remote from the outside world. In fact at times like this it gave you quite a jolt to realise there were other people out there carrying on with their own lives.

The corn harvest was good for me this year, as my knowledge of tractor driving now came to the fore. Although I had not cut a field of corn as yet, after instructions from the farmer about the intricate movements at the field corners – where you had to make a wide sweep with the tractor to enable you to be in position to cut the next tier. It was a delightful job, the sun shining and the fruits of your labour spread out behind you.

The man on the binder behind would call out from time to time to make conversation, but it was difficult to hear what he said above the noise of the engine. The farmer's wives did us proud. During harvest time they would arrive at break times with baskets loaded up with food and cold drinks, meat pies, apple tarts, cake and buttered scones, always freshly cooked and straight from the oven. These women were always hard at work around the farm, milking, feeding the live stock and in their kitchens, and they always managed to smile and give you a cheery word. They were indeed the salt of the earth.

On hearing that the hot fine weather was about to break and he still had a couple more fields to cut, the farmer asked if we would be willing to work on into the evening, to finish carrying in the corn from the field we had been working on that day. We agreed, saying we would hitch-hike back when the work was finished. We rang the hostel to cancel our transport and told the warden not to worry about our meals as the farmer would be providing these before the evening's work began.

Resuming work, looking at the amount of corn that was left in the field, we had a few misgivings. It seemed we had taken on a marathon task; it was late evening before the last trailer load was brought in.

Wearily walking back along the main road, with quite a good few miles to go, a shooting brake stopped, offering us a lift. Apologising for our dusty clothes we thankfully climbed in. Our good samaritans told us they were holiday makers touring Devon, and asked why we were out so late. We explained, and they were astonished when they realised we had just completed a fourteen hour day. They were most interested to hear about our life in the Land Army. They asked endless questions and were eager to tell their friends about us when they got home. Very nicely, they diverted from their route to take us right to the hostel door. Thanking them profusely for their kindness, they replied it had been a pleasure, as meeting us had really made their day. A hot bath and climbing into bed with a warm drink made ours.

Percy the bull was a very amiable sort of creature who lived at a particular farm where I was to spend, at intervals over the months, many working days. I was rather wary when I first saw him in a field, but the farmer assured me that he was quiet enough, specially when he was mixed in with the herd of cows. The geese however were a different matter, at least one of them was – a large gander who was extremely vicious. He had only to spy you attempting to go into the yard and out he would come, wings flapping, neck arched, hissing loudly, almost spitting venom, so we always approached this part of the farm with utmost caution.

We were doing exactly this one day, and breathing a sigh of relief, when he appeared from somewhere too close for comfort and we dashed into a barn slamming the door behind us. With this dreadful bird waiting outside ready to pounce, we were in that barn for nearly half an hour before the farmer came to let us out, with Frankie, my workmate, holding on to the back of my coat with grim desperation.

That same afternoon I had to go into the yard alone. Percy the bull was wandering around his enclosure. I heard the gander arriving and, knowing he would be blocking the entrance to the field I was going to, I had to make a split second decision. Was I to call the big gander's bluff or take a chance that Percy was as quiet as the farmer said he was? I chose Percy, who looked mildly surprised, but uninterested, at the being who had climbed the gate and crashed through his pen and over the other gate like greased lightning.

Micky, the warden's dog, was a shaggy-coated terrier type mongrel. Very quick and alert, he liked joining in any rumpus that was going on. Without doubt his favourite game was when Flo stood at the top of the stair, while I held him down the bottom. She would call "Micky, Micky, Micky," and he would run up to her at incredible speed. As soon as he reached the top stair, I would call him down again. This would go on at great length until he was literally sliding down the stairs. When we'd had enough, we would sit on the hall floor with Micky panting, his eyes bright, still raring to go, until the warden came out of her office to call him in saying he's had his exercise for the day.

Whenever either Flo or I came in from work, as soon as we got inside the door, we would make a high pitched yodelling noise that carried right up to the top floor. If a reply came back we would know the other was in.

One evening an argument ensued, a rare event, but on principle neither me or Flo would admit we were in the wrong. This led to days of ignoring each other until the warden sent for us to ask why should such good friends be like this, and if it was not settled pretty quickly she would be banging our heads together. This broke the ice and we had to laugh. The warden smiled and said, "Thank goodness that's all over – I just couldn't stand the quietness of the hostel a day longer."

Deciding at last to write to John, I explained in the best way I knew how, my feelings about everything, hoping he would somehow understand. I assured him there wasn't anyone else, but I felt I wanted the freedom to choose, should I want, to go out with anyone without feeling guilty, even though they may just be a casual acquaintance.

A week later I went to meet Pete, to see Timmy, but he was alone. I could see by the look on his face there was something wrong. He told me Timmy had been losing his appetite, finally refusing to eat and drink, and had several fits within a week. The vet had decided it would be advisable to have him put down. I felt a deep sense of loss at the news, but realised it had been the kindest thing to do under the circumstances. I didn't really feel like attending the dance that night, so I stayed in the bar with the old couple at the inn, and had a quiet evening, having a drink and talking to them.

The following week however, I did go to the dance. Near the end someone told me that John had just walked in. I went over to speak to him only to find he had not yet received my letter. I explained what I had written, and he didn't seem very pleased about this. I didn't really expect him to be, but after more discussion we agreed to meet the following day to talk it over.

Watching him walk towards me next day I thought how smart he looked, he really was nice. We talked for quite a long time. On parting he asked if I would write to him during the week to let him know whether I would reconsider and see him again.

It was mid-week before I wrote to tell him I would see him again. The annual September Fair had arrived in the town and I already had intentions of going there on the Saturday night, so I told John in the letter if he called at the hostel we could go to the fair together.

I waited until nine thirty, then made up my mind to go to the fair, meeting the rest of the girls, as it looked unlikely he would turn up as late as this. Going to the fair was great fun, and made a nice change from the usual weekend. About an hour before it closed at midnight, I saw John making his way through the crowd. I was quite surprised to realise I was really pleased to see him.

Evidently the person who had given him a lift had been rather later than planned. I felt sorry that after he had made such an effort to get there, there was only a short time before I had to go back to the hostel. John promised to call for me the following Wednesday, and I assured him I would be in Torrington the next weekend. We kept to this arrangement until his leave ended, it seemed all the doubt in my mind had cleared, and I would be quite content to resume letter writing until his army service ended in six month's time.

Friday nights were routine, spending an hour in the laundry room pressing our clothes for the weekend. This was done with great care, soaping the seams in our trousers to give knife sharp creases, and ironing our tops and dresses to perfection as it was nice to look good after we had been in working clothes all week.

Having done this, we would make our way to the milk bar for our weekly treat, taking a great deal of time choosing whether to have a knickerbocker glory, banana split, or select a milkshake in our favourite flavour. We would then sit at the tables for a good hour, discussing different subjects and enjoying our choice of drink.

I had decided some time ago to save all my sweet coupons (which was the only way you could purchase sweets in those days) to make up a parcel to send to my stepmother for her birthday. I took care to make a selection I knew she would like, and it gave me great pleasure to pack them up and post them off as it had meant months of sweetless days for me. I received a letter thanking me for her card, so I replied asking whether she enjoyed the sweets. It seems they never arrived. I was so disappointed, but there was little I could do about it, except to hope the person who stole them suffered an agonising toothache.

Pat had been in the Land Army for nine months and was really loving the life, however, having joined illegally at the age of sixteen, giving a false date of birth, she was waiting in rather an agitated state for a letter to arrive from Head Office to say she had been found out.

She had a visit from an official who told her she had done a very serious thing by breaking the law in this manner and she would most certainly be sent home. She sent a letter the following day to plead her case, very apologetic, saying how much she enjoyed the work, and that she had only thought how best to serve her country by joining, (anything to save being sacked). Obviously this show of patriotism worked, as the reply came to say that seeing as how she would soon be seventeen, and the damage had already been done, she would be allowed to stay after all. This was greeted with great relief, and we celebrated her birthday by going to an Air Force dance at the local base, all Pat's worries over. I believe there were many girls who had done the same thing, and great credit was due to them to tackle the hard work at such a tender age.

As autumn approached, the many different colours of leaves, the gold russets and browns mingling together, made a wonderful scene as we rode along the country lanes. Although by now we should have been used to all this over the years, it still gave us pleasure to see it all.

As the darker evenings closed in we found ourselves spending more time together around the fire, playing cards or just talking about almost every subject of interest there was to talk about.

It would have been thought by now that the enthusiasm I had for the life I was living and for the endless days of work would have waned a little, but this was certainly not so. But it wasn't all sweetness and light all the time. This extreme cold, especially on the high ground of the coastal farms, was at times almost unbearable when pulling root crops of sugar beet or swedes. We had spent a day doing this and returned the next to load them onto trailers.

The wind was icy so we sat in the hedge to try to ward it off a little. The farmer had left the tractor and trailer in the field overnight, to make an early start, which wasn't a very clever idea at all as he found out when it wouldn't start. We sat for over an hour, occasionally jumping up to do warming exercises. As time went on we were totally numb with cold, and in the end we were wishing it wouldn't start at all.

Sure enough our wishes came true – the farmer had given up at last. Although we realised they would still be there tomorrow, it was good to phone in for the lorry and get back to the warmth of the hostel to thaw out.

We didn't mind the cold so much when threshing, as there was much more movement, and most times we were in a much more sheltered place. Many times out in the open fields if it started to rain you would be soaked through. Sitting in the lorry on the way home with the steam rising from your knees due to the warmth of your body, all you could so was hope there was plenty of hot water for a bath when you got in.

Very often girls would get out of bed in the morning and leave their pyjama trousers on for extra warmth under their dungarees, but in the end they would just find they had two pairs of trousers to wash and dry instead of one. However, we survived all the hard winters and seemed to be none the worse because of them.

It was during one of these cold spells that Moira and I were sent to clear the upstairs loft area of a barn, piling the straw bales into neater stacks, sweeping the floors to gather all the loose pieces together. This was good as it was much warmer in there than outside, but we were warned not to jump around too much as the floor was not too safe.

We were chattering away as we worked, when there was a loud crack and I suddenly found myself suspended between floors, holding on grimly by my elbows with a long drop below me. Moira dashed over to grab me and at that moment the farmer walked into the barn. He looked as shaken as I felt, but I assured him I wasn't badly hurt. Sitting on the floor some time later examining the scratches and scrapes on my arms, I looked up and stared in disbelief at them both as they sat together on a straw bale. Moira had tears rolling down her cheeks and the farmer was red-faced trying to stifle the laughter as she related how one minute I was there and then I wasn't, while he was saying, "I couldn't believe my eyes when I walked in and saw a pair of legs in wellies dangling in mid air."

I sat and looked at them. My face must have registered my thoughts as the farmer said soberly, "We know it was no laughing matter maid, it could have been very nasty," and burst into laughter once more exclaiming, "but I haven't seen anything so funny in years." Oh well, I thought, if you can't beat 'em, better join 'em, and so I joined in their laughter.

The latest letter from John had said that his Mother would like me to call in one Sunday for tea when I was in Torrington, so that she could meet me in person. Although I was in no way shy with people, it seemed a daunting prospect to just go to someone's house and introduce myself. It took three more letters asking me to go before I decided to do it.

I knew he had three sisters and four brothers. One I had already met while out with John, and I had worked with his father on the WAEC while threshing on the moor – he was also working for them at the time, although neither of us had given any recognition to the fact that we both knew John. I hoped that there would not be too many of the family there for my first visit.

His mother, answering my knock on the door, welcomed me warmly and introduced me to his brother Cyril and sister Ruby who was visiting with her husband. He recognised me at once because he was a threshing contractor I had worked with on several occasions when the farmers had hired his machinery. Naturally enough I was asked many questions about myself, where I came from, how many were in my family, all the usual things people want to know at the first meeting.

It turned out to be a most pleasant evening. We had a very lavish tea where I was cajoled into eating far more than I needed. It must have been when I told them what was in our pack each day and they thought they would feed me enough to last me for the rest of the week. When I left, John's parents asked me to visit them again, saying that I would be most welcome at any time. I assured them that I would and left with a small sigh of relief on finding it hadn't been so bad after all. I even started looking forward to the next visit.

After a few more visits I was asked to spend my Christmas leave there; a time which turned out to be most enjoyable.

CHAPTER SEVEN

As I danced my way around the tree in the square to welcome in 1949, little did I know that this was going to be a year of great change for me, and would mean a good deal of travelling to new places.

Meanwhile, life in the hostel and on the farms went on as usual, although I was sent to do a job, accompanied by another girl, which was really incredibly hard work and which I had not tackled before. This was cleaning out a calf house where the young animals had been reared after being weaned away from their mothers. The straw and manure was about three feet high and had been solidly trampled under foot; the only way to move it was to dig in the fork and try to roll it off in layers with both of us pushing it out of the door to pile it into the yard. It was not often we felt like giving up on a job, but this time we would have done so gladly. At the end of the three days it took to complete it, we were very near to tears. It was with great relief we said goodbye to the place, hoping it would be a long time before we had to do this again. It hadn't helped either that a calf in the next shed had been separated from its mother on our first day there. The cow was in the field next to the shed and was mooing loudly with the calf answering back almost incessantly the whole time we were there. It felt like the start of a holiday, climbing into the lorry the next day to go back to more normal working conditions.

The months of February and March were very similar to other years; sorting endless barns full of potatoes, hedging and threshing.

Lesley had been made work duty supervisor, doling out the work rota as fairly as she could. Although she still kept her easy going manner while off duty, anyone trying to cash in on the friendship basis by asking to be sent to the better farms were quickly given a sharp reprimand and told in no uncertain terms to go and do the job they were given. Although this was greeted by a few with animosity the majority agreed she had the right attitude for the job.

Waking one very cold morning we found there was no running water in the wash rooms. For some unknown reason the stop taps outside had been turned off and so the only running water was from a tap in the yard. Washing took no time at all – we didn't linger out there too long. This was the reason for me sitting in the lorry quite early, quietly minding my own business and contemplating the day's work ahead, when out came the chargehand who looked at me then staggered back in a mock attempt to faint, shouting "Look who's here everyone, she's on time for a change." I stared at her for a while, most surprised, as I had never been a latecomer, then I felt very mutinous indeed.

I climbed out of the lorry and went back inside the hostel. While she tried cajole me into coming out, I waited until everyone was on board and then gave it another five minutes just to add a little more weight to my protest. I then walked slowly out and climbed in without a word, while the girls who had witnessed all this had sat there (as they related afterwards) with baited breath to see how long it would be before I came out. They greeted my arrival with a loud cheer, although I was still angry for quite a time afterwards, but I must confess on reflection I had rather enjoyed it all.

Spring was just around the corner once again, and in such a beautiful area as this, it was something to really look forward to. It would also be only a few weeks before John would be home and out of the army for good. To add to all this I was sent to a farm for general duties, and was booked to be there for several weeks.

The family were very homely with two delightful young children, the farmer and his wife were quite young and I immediately felt at ease with them and quickly fitted in with the daily routine. I loved feeding the young calves; going into the shed with a bucket of warm milk, they would nearly knock you over in their eagerness to be fed. Immersing your hand into the milk with only fingertips showing, they would greedily suck up the milk, their very rough tongues rasping against your fingers.

In a field at the top of the lane was a tame lamb that had been hand-reared in the farm house but was now old enough to join the others on grass. Each morning she would run to the iron fence as the lorry stopped, and greet me in her bleating calls until I bent down to stroke her little woolly head and speak to her. The other girls in the lorry started to get quite interested in the morning ritual, and called her Titch, after me. Each day they would say, "Look, she's waiting for you again."

It became something that was looked forward to and gave us a happy start to the day.

As the weeks went on, I was getting more accustomed to working there and was really happy. One day the farmer asked if I would go into the house and talk with him and his wife. It seemed that they wanted me to leave the hostel and go to live with them on a permanent basis. They did not want an answer right away, but gave me time to think about it.

What an enormous decision I had to make now, and it had to be a very careful one. Seeing the hopeful look on their faces when they asked me made it more than difficult, especially as, through working with them I became to like them very much. However, I had to remember that John was on his way home and if I moved to the farm I would be living too far away to be able to see him, and it would mean severing my ties with all the girls and the Land Army. If after a while things didn't work out at the farm, as sometime happens even with the best of intentions, I would be left high and dry not knowing where to go next. I finally decided against a change, but with very mixed feelings. The farmer and his wife were disappointed when I told them, but understood my reasons and left the offer open should I change my mind at a later date.

Lambing time meant weeks of very little rest for the farmer. It was not unusual for him to be working through the night until dawn keeping the flock under close observation, watching out for the sheep who would be in difficulties giving birth to her offspring.

It was really enjoyable when we walked around the field, helping to check them, and seeing a ewe with her lamb by her side stamping her feet to warn us off. Another danger to watch out for was a ewe grazing on a flat surfaced field, lying on her back, unable to roll over due to the weight of the lamb beside her. She would not survive if left in this position for long, and for this reason farmers would put them on sloping ground when possible. Many times when travelling to work, we would stop the lorry and climb a gate to assist the ewes, and I would, without hesitation, do the same today.

Most sheep were very caring mothers, but there were the odd one or two who completely rejected their lamb and would butt it away each time it approached. There was very little could be done about this, but to take the lamb into the farm house to be bottle fed, or place a coat of a more unfortunate lamb over its back hoping that mother would accept it as her own. Luckily, nine times out of ten she would, which made it a much easier situation for all concerned.

Unknown to us as we travelled to work to go hoeing, this was going to be a very strange day. The severe drought we were having at the time had made the ground rock hard and we could just about scratch the top of it. We always kept our hoes sharpened to make it easier, but this had done little to improve the job under these conditions.

The heat was intense during the afternoon, the air strangely silent, when we heard a long droning noise. Looking up, we saw a swarm of bees flying in a perfect V formation just above our heads. Suddenly from out of the clear blue sky, large drops of rain began to fall. It was so unexpected, we just stood there. The ground seemed to sizzle under this sudden down pour and within minutes we were soaked to the skin.

A deafening thunderclap sent us rushing to the nearest hedge where we huddled as the storm raged on. It was quite awesome and continued for nearly an hour, then as it cleared the sun started to shine down again and, except for the wet ground and our soaked clothes, it was as if nothing had happened.

The most uncanny thing was, girls in different areas had no experience of this at all.

Luckily the weather did break after this, to the relief of the farmers who had suffered great difficulty in the very dry spell, but as I mentioned, it had been a very strange day.

I ran down the hostel stairs having been told I was wanted on the phone. I wondered who could be calling, then I heard John's voice telling me he was home. This was a surprise as I hadn't known exactly when he would be back. He told me he would be coming over that evening to see me. I dashed to get ready as I wanted to look my best for the occasion.

One of the girls ran into my room saying, "Your boyfriend is downstairs, all the girls are taking a look at him, he's just like a film star." I hurried down knowing he would be most embarrassed with everyone trying to take a peek at him. Sure enough there he stood looking very ill at ease, so I quickly ushered him outside. He had brought me a beautiful manicure set all laid in deep blue velvet, and also a gift which was the envy of everyone – two pairs of sheer seamed nylon stockings. These were unobtainable in this country, except at an exorbitant price on the black market, or from abroad.

Later in the evening I told him about the chance I had to live on the farm. He said he wouldn't have tried to help me to decide, but was glad I had made the decision he liked best. Then we discussed his future, when his demob leave ended. Before he went into the Army he was a fireman on the steam railway, and his job had been kept open for him, so he hoped to be able to go back to this. The odd working hours would make things awkward to make regular dates to go places, but seeing as I would be staying at his home most weekends, this meant I would at least be there when he was, so it seemed things could work out quite well, anyway it was good he was home at last. There was little danger of us getting tired of seeing each other, and there would be plenty to talk about when we did, it seemed everything was going to work out fine.

A brewery owner had a large field of strawberries, and employed us to pick them. When we arrived and presented ourselves at the rather large and imposing house, his smartly dressed wife answered the door to instruct us as to where we would find the baskets to collect the fruit.

Her face was a picture as she surveyed the cluster of girls waiting at the door. I must admit we probably looked a motley crew in our well-worn dungarees and hair tied up in our cloth turbans, but we didn't really warrant the look she gave us, as if she had just encountered a heap of rotting manure on her doorstep. With a curt "don't eat the strawberries while you are picking them," she pointed to the field and firmly closed the door on us.

It was a good hour past breaktime when we realised no tea was forthcoming. An argument ensued as to who was going to ask for it. After a while, three of us decided to go together, to give each other moral support.

On hearing our request, and looking angrier than ever, she said, "Good Heavens, don't tell me I have to provide drinks as well as pay for you."

It took a great amount of courage to explain it was written in the contract she had received. And our bravery would have earned us a medal when we informed her that we would be back after mid-day for more.

We didn't eat the strawberries; seeing that the large windows of the house gave a full view of the field, we just didn't dare.

Chapter Eight

The ability to make changes in my lifestyle, even though I would be content with whatever I was doing at the time, was second nature to me. This was proved on hearing there was a vacancy at the school for learner drivers. I immediately applied as opportunities like this were very rare. With so many girls going for the same spot, there seemed little hope so I put it to the back of my mind and almost forgot about it. It was quite a shock when I received a letter to say I had been accepted.

Travelling down in the van with the driver who had been allotted to take me to Newton Abbot in South Devon, I had to pinch myself to make sure I wasn't just dreaming, and wondered what I had let myself in for this time.

The camp, with many large huts built over a wide area, was the living quarters for the girls working in that district. I was placed in one of these for the three weeks of my stay there.

The girls were very nice, but as I only mixed with them at night I didn't really fit in with the true camaraderie there, but it was still quite pleasant.

Ernie, the driving instructor, was a no-nonsense fellow and made it quite clear that I was there to learn to drive as quickly and efficiently as possible. If I showed no promise by the end of a full week I would be out on my ear; it was too expensive to be otherwise.

After a morning around the camp, being shown gear changing, clutch and brakes, we went onto the roads. He said, "Let's see if you can drive in a straight line." As I was happily driving along he suddenly yelled, "Where do you think we ruddy well are – in America?" As I glanced at him he exploded, "If you prefer to drive on the wrong side of the road, go ahead, but don't expect me to sit here with you."

He showed me a small stick he kept beside him. If after seven days I was still grating the gears, he told me I would be getting a sharp tap across my knuckles until I got it right. Every day was a battle of wills. One day he stopped me on a steep hill and got out, saying "I'm placing my very expensive watch behind the back wheel. If you run back as you pull away it will take you a year to pay for it." I made certain that I didn't. To this day I don't know for certain if the watch had been there or not, but now I'm older and wiser, I doubt it.

As I began to gain more confidence, I really started to enjoy driving. Ernie had dropped his stern attitude, and on the last day he let me drive to Buckfast Abbey to look around, saying we had both deserved a day's holiday and he would be seeing me again soon to take me for my test in Torquay.

Back in Barnstaple, I was proud to be able to show off my driving skills, but had to suffer the hilarity that ensued as everyone watched me propping up the legs of the seat with blocks so that I could see through the windscreen properly.

Some weeks later I was sent to the Instow hotel for a short stay. As their driver had a wrist injury, I drove the girls to work whilst she, as a qualified driver, sat beside me.

Being right on the sea front, it was nice to look out of the window in the early morning and see the view of the sea, and to just go across to take a leisurely stroll along the fine sandy beach at night.

One of the first girls I got to know was Rose, who met me at the door. She was very friendly and made me feel at home right away, little did we know that in later years we would come into contact again.

On my return to Barnstaple, the date for my driving test came through. I was to go down the day before, the driver was told to wait in case I didn't pass. On arriving, I sat in my van waiting for Ernie, and saw him approaching looking absolutely furious with a girl trainee driver walking sheepishly behind him. He ordered her to get in, and without as much as a "good morning" he said, "Drive on, let's get this sorted out." What 'this' was I didn't dare ask. He told me to turn into a street and stop, then told me to do a three point turn. I took far more turns than this to get the van around, seeing as how he had picked the narrowest street he could find, but I managed to do this manoeuvre to near perfection. With a very smug look on his face, he turned to the girl who looked as if she wished the floor would swallow her up, and said, "There, now you're a witness." She managed a very weak nod in agreement.

Eventually calming down, he explained. A girl he had taught had made such a mess of her test in the three point turn that she had informed the tester she had never been shown how to do this – information which had been reported to Head Office. Ernie had been given a severe reprimand which must have been a great blow to his pride. He apologised later for using me as an outlet for his anger. I readily forgave him as, to my mind, he was the best instructor anyone could have had. To make him feel better I told him so.

Waiting outside the testing office I saw the man emerge from the door looking very forbidding with a hard starched collar, pin-striped suit and bowler hat – most officious. I immediately tensed and, although I seemed to drive quite well, he failed me on carelessly not looking to the left on two occasions. Ernie was very sympathetic but surprised as he thought I would have sailed through.

My second test turned out to be very unusual. This time I was to stay with the school for a week, and the driver returned to Barnstaple with a truck going that way. The same tester took me, but I was determined not to let nerves get the better of me. Halfway through the test he told me to pull over and stop. What on earth had I done wrong now?

"Well young lady," he said, "what was wrong with you last time? Today your driving is as different as chalk from cheese." He added that I could drive back to the centre as there was no need to continue the test. Ernie looked concerned at our early arrival and dashed over to the van, but the tester said, "Don't worry, she passed with flying colours this time."

I was puzzled when he sat for some time making no attempt to get out of the van until he said, "I have always wanted to have a go at driving one of these – would it be alright?" Ernie and I glanced at each other, quite surprised, as I climbed into the back. He didn't do very well at all as he veered the van too close to a wall, scraping the wing. "I hope this never gets out," he said laughing, "or I'll never live it down." It seemed funny. I had been so much in awe of him, when he was really a jolly old chap after all.

Ernie said, "When we get back, go and have some lunch, and then you will be free to go back to Barnstaple." This was a thought that had never entered my head; that after passing my test I would be expected to drive the sixty miles back quite alone, just an hour after qualifying. Talk about being thrown in at the deep end. Taking a deep breath and summoning all the courage I could muster, I started off, arriving home tired but exhilarated, feeling I had just passed the greatest test of all.

Being a driver meant getting up much earlier in the mornings in order to take the ten minute walk to collect the van from the garage, checking the oil, water and tyres (this was a must, we were told), and parking up outside the hostel before breakfast. Then you needed to check the list to find out where you had to drop all the girls, making sure you ended up at the farm where you were working that day, and then pick them all up again on the way home.

I was in my element now as I really loved driving along the country lanes with the usual chorus of songs in the background. The one thing I had not taken into account was that, on becoming a driver, I had signed to say I would be willing to be transferred anywhere I may be needed. That time had now arrived.

I was to be moved to Crediton in mid-Devon, and another girl was needed in the same area. Flo, who some time ago had parted from her long time boyfriend and had met a young farmer, declined. In the end it was Evelyn, who had moved from Torrington with us, who decided to accompany me.

I really hated the thought of leaving Barnstaple where I had been really happy, but had no choice. We loaded up our belongings and set off for Crediton. We were to be in private lodgings, no hostel there. I took Evelyn to hers first; this was a council house where she was to stay with a man and wife and two children.

Then I started the search for my lodgings. It turned out to be in a small back alley, a tiny house with a kitchen where we ate our meals and a narrow adjoining scullery which I discovered was the place I was to bathe, in a tin bath filled with hot water from kettles warmed on the grate. The bedroom was the worst of all though; just large enough to hold one bed with our clothes to be hung on hooks around the wall, and, to my horror, I was told I was to share the bed with another girl who was lodging there.

It was very late when I decided to go to bed and I was woken when the other girl came in. After introducing herself, she amazed me by relating for the next hour her conquests with all the different men she had met. I wondered how anyone could do this without finding out the type of person they were confiding in. It was quite a revelation.

Knowing there were difficulties in finding lodgings, I said nothing at the time, deciding to try and make the best of it and spending my evenings with Evelyn at her lodge. However, when I walked in one night to find my supper laid out on the kitchen table being thoroughly enjoyed by several mice, I decided enough was enough, and asked to be found some-where else to live.

In the end, room was made for me at the same place as Evelyn, which was a lot more comfortable. We were expected to help with the housework and to baby-sit most evenings as our landlady and her husband both worked in a factory on evening shifts. On Wednesday nights John would arrive with Evelyn's boyfriend who owned a motor bike, and we would go our separate ways to spend time alone with them. On one of these visits we decided to get engaged and I was given a ring in an alleyway where we could hear the band from the dance hall playing our favourite tune. It was quite romantic, but I wished we had been back in the hostel where I could have celebrated with the girls there.

Lesley wrote me a most ridiculous letter which took hours to read as it was written on yards of toilet paper and did a lot to cheer me up. Evelyn and I admitted we were both happier when we were told we were to return to Barnstaple and resume our work there.

On our return I was amazed to hear that Flo had gone home one weekend, got married to her farmer, and no one seemed to know her whereabouts. It must seem rather odd now to think that close friends would just do things without telling the other, but that was the way of life. It was just the sheer independence of doing your own thing no matter what, taking opportunities as they came, and accepting without question other people's decisions. However, I was to meet up with Flo again much later.

A lady had, in admiration of the work done by the girls of the Land Army, left a small sum of money for us to buy something for the hostel which we could all share.

Two girls were sent out to make a purchase. We left the decision to them, and were surprised when they returned with a framed picture of Van Gough's *Sunflowers*. Not being very art minded at the time, we were not all that appreciative of their choice, nevertheless it was placed on the wall for all to see.

Standing alone in the lounge one morning studying the picture, I heard the announcer on the wireless say that the Women's Land Army was to be disbanded in the new year. I hoped that I had not heard this right, but the warden came in to me and said, "Did you hear the news just then?" and I realised it was true.

She called all the girls together and told them. The news was greeted with the same dismay as I had felt, it seemed like the bottom had dropped out of the world. There was still a shortage of food in the country and we did not understand the reason for disbanding the Land Army, but the powers that be had decided, and had left hundreds of very unhappy people who really loved this life on the land, with a very dim view of the future.

Some weeks later I was told that a farmer near Torrington had enquired if any girl would be interested in finishing off the months left in the Land Army to live in with his family and work on his farm. Not wishing to see the final closing down of the hostel I jumped at the chance, at least I would still be doing the thing I liked best. My farming days would not be over after all, many of the girls I had served with in the Torrington Hostel had married and settled there, and with John's home only three miles from the farm, it seemed that for me at least, things were going to turn out well.

CHAPTER NINE

Walking into the roomy farmhouse kitchen of Belle View Farm, two pairs of eyes stared at me with much curiosity. These belonged to the two young children who were introduced as Margaret and Donald. The farmer I was to call Ron, while his wife was always Mrs Easterbrook.

There was great excitement as the children were told to take me to my room to unpack. This was a comfortable and homely room with a large bed, small dresser and wardrobe. After the children had departed I started to place my few belongings in the appropriate places. This took no time at all, I seemed to have acquired little more than when I had started out in 1946, but this was of no concern to me, compared to the wealth of experience I had gained, along with the friends I had spent those years with.

I was to find that life on a private farm was to be very time consuming. Just a cup of tea on rising at 6.30 am, then a long walk across the fields to bring in the cows for the morning's milking, which at this time was done by hand. There were about fourteen cows in all, including Clara, a rather scraggy creature who was treated by all the family with loving care. She was the first cow they had owned on first buying the farm. After milking, the calves then demanded attention to be fed from the buckets of fresh milk, and then I had my long-awaited breakfast.

On my first morning I was rather put out to go out to work without eating first, but soon found delight in working up a real healthy appetite and then going into the warm kitchen to find plates full with home cured bacon, fresh eggs and home baked bread, with rolls covered in cream topped with jam to follow. A feast indeed. There was little need to worry about diet as all this would be worked off during the morning.

The first task after breakfast would be to take the cows back to the field accompanied by the dogs, who thoroughly enjoyed herding them along, then return to the yard to feed the hens, collect eggs, and fill the pail with slops to feed the pigs. There was no easy way to do this, as you had to slide down a muddy slope trying to keep the contents of the pail intact while the ever-hungry sows were waiting to crowd around, knocking over the food that had not already been spilled.

This was the routine each day, to be followed by field work as the season demanded: planting seeds, dropping and lifting potatoes, hoeing, hay and corn harvest. All this was followed by a repeat of the morning routine, but always finishing up with a huge meal at the end of the day, eaten with great relish.

Vince was a dairy worker who spent every hour of his spare time at the farm. A bachelor, he made it his second home and we worked together on all the jobs around the farm; he was an amusing and cheerful companion. As well as the farmer's children Donald and Margaret, there was also, in the holidays and at weekends, a school friend of Donald's who for some unknown reason was nicknamed Bucket. Although he would help with the chores, his greatest ability was to assist Donald in getting into mischief, with Margaret trailing in their wake, seeing how it was all done.

On some evenings John, who had now left the railway to work for contractors, would bring his lorry, and having nowhere else to go we would sit in the cab. One night there were the three of them crouched in the back of the lorry, hands over their mouths to muffle the sound. The surprise on their faces was something to behold when asked what they were doing and were yanked bodily and without ceremony over the side. It became a standing joke with the family and the three pranksters, and both John and myself saw it as a bit of harmless fun.

However, there was one time I didn't condone bad behaviour. I had gone into town to spend a Sunday evening, and on my return I noticed that a small furry monkey I owned and which had hung in pride of place above my bed wherever I had lived, had been taken down and its face pressed in. On learning that the culprit had been Donald, I immediately put him across my knee and gave him a spanking with my slipper. I awaited with some trepidation for the reaction of his parents to this, but I need not have worried, they fully agreed I was right. As for Donald, he was most apologetic and we carried on as before, the best of mates.

Farming had many hazards, especially when using machinery. I was at the bottom of a field where Ron was disc harrowing. This was an implement with round blades used for slicing through the earth. He told me to jump up behind him on the tractor and he would give me a lift to the top of the field. Halfway up I lost my footing and fell to the ground. I froze as I saw the discs coming towards me. It was at the same moment Ron looked round and slammed on the brake, coming to a halt. I don't know which of us was more shocked, but he was to say many times later he hadn't a clue what made him suddenly turn around, but we were both thankful that he did.

It was time for the steers to be brought in from the fields, but I didn't realise that they were in a place down in the valley near the milk factory on the other side of town. This would mean driving them up the steep street through the town, and the three miles back to the farm. Ron took me down there by car and left me to get on with it.

What I didn't realise was that half way up the steep street was an alley that led back to the place I had just fetched them from. Sure enough they found it, and back they went. I eventually found a willing helper who was prepared to wait by the gap while I drove them up once again. Waiting at the farm was Ron with a sort of half grin on his face, asking me where I had been, adding that I should have been back an hour ago. Seeing the look on my face he said, "I suppose they disappeared when you went up the hill," his grin getting wider. Hot and tired, I was not amused, but all he said was, "Never mind, you'll be wiser next time." To which I replied, "I'll be so much wiser – I shall get someone else to go."

It had been a heavy work day. I sank thankfully into bed and felt like staying there for a week – very wishful thinking.

I was surprised when I was woken much earlier than usual by Ron who asked me to fetch the cows and start the milking in order to get it done in time for the dairy collection; as I would be doing it on my own today it would take much longer, but he added, "Missis will be out to help when she can." It appeared Ron had been up all night with a very difficult calving, and wanted a couple of hours sleep before seeing to the rest of the chores.

I admonished him for not calling me to help, but he said he didn't like waking me and it was better that I was rested to take on the work next day, but I would have liked to have been there to see it all.

It was the large yard outside the shippen that gave me concern, as it was about two feet deep in mud and slurry and was difficult to walk through each day. I complained on several occasions about this and should have known better than to offer to help clear it, but offer I did.

Armed with buckets and a wooden-sided cart, we started to scoop up the mess, the children joined in amid much laughter which climbed to a crescendo as I came around the side and Ron, on the point of throwing a bucketful into the cart, missed his aim. The whole lot landed on me. Their only regret was that we had no camera at the time to record it.

Being in no fit state to walk into the kitchen, I had to hose down first in the shippen before I was able to go inside for a bath. Everyone else had a delightful time telling all and sundry what a mess I had looked and what great fun it had been. Somehow I wasn't in complete agreement with them, but it was a great joy to all when the yard was cleared and we were able to walk easily on the dry flat surface.

One job I really liked was taking the churns of milk in the small trailer down to the milk factory. These contained the watery skimmed milk left over after it had been scalded from making clotted cream. This was saved up until there was enough to send down to the dairy who re-sold it to anyone needing it for pig-feed. It was great to be driving again, if only for a few miles, and good to feel the busy atmosphere of a large factory, being greeted by many of the local workers who still remembered me from the Torrington Hostel.

The only other time I drove the car was to take the children to Sunday school at the village church each Sunday afternoon. I usually had to listen to them arguing all the way there and back, mainly as to which one would sit in the front seat beside me. I soon resolved this by letting them take it in turns each week, but nevertheless they still found something else to disagree about. I soon found the best way to deal with this was to ignore them altogether and pretend they just weren't there.

As the herd arrived at the gate waiting for me to take them in for milking, I noticed one was missing. I took the rest of them in and told Ron I would go back and look for her. I spied her near the hedge at the bottom of the field and saw she had a new born calf with her. I ran back excitedly into the farmhouse to break the good news to everyone. They were all so pleased, especially as it was a heifer calf which could be reared to become a milker, thus increasing the herd.

I was told that the milk from a cow which had just calved was very rich and would be turned into cream; the milk placed in bowls and allowed to stand until all the fats settled thickly on top and then slowly simmered until the thick rich cream clotted and could be scooped into large dishes for eating.

Going into the kitchen, I sat down for my meal and Mrs Easterbrook, with a broad smile on her face, placed the huge bowl of cream in front of me and said, "That belongs to you as the first person to find the calf gets the cream." To say I was delighted was an understatement. Naturally I left it in the dairy room for all to share, but I proudly presented a dish of the cream to John's family where I related how it had all come about. It seemed to me this was a lovely custom, but still wonder if it was invented by this very kind family for my benefit alone, as this was the sort of thing they would do. Whichever way it was, it made me feel good.

Ron and his wife had to go away over a weekend to a farming conference, leaving me to run the farm aided by Vince, Bucket and the children, with instructions to start digging up the potatoes in the field. The tractor, an old Alice Charmer, was at most times difficult to work with, but this day refused to start and I wasted a whole morning messing with it, which did little to aid my temper. Prior to this, things seemed to have got off to a bad start from the word go.

Maud, one of the cows who was of very uncertain temperament, decided this was the day to be on her worst behaviour. While I was milking her she continually kicked out so I decided to rope her back legs. I was just about to do this when she stepped back, putting her hoof firmly in the bucket of milk, finally kicking it over. That was her milk yield gone for that morning.

After bedding down the animals, I had to think about preparing meals for the other four hungry mouths and myself. Amid taunts of "Mother don't cook it like that," and the occasional grunt of "Yuk," as they were eating, I coped – but only just – and told them they were darned lucky to get anything at all.

I was thankful to see the boss return, even though I had a ticking off for the small amount of potatoes that had been dug, which I explained was the tractor's fault not mine. I just hoped it would be a long time before they decided to go away again.

Mrs Easterbrook was very amused at the complaints against my cooking, and probably pleased they appreciated hers so much. My thought on the subject was that she was more than welcome to it, I'd stick with what I knew best.

As Christmas approached, preparations became hectic with orders arriving for chickens and geese. We spent long evenings in the shed outside plucking the feathers, then sending them on into the kitchen to be gutted and tied to look presentable for the customers. It seemed endless and was a job that made you feel very itchy and grubby.

We still kept a number of geese though, and these always wandered around the yard in front of the house, as Ron said, they were even better watchdogs than the dogs as they made loud honking sounds if they were disturbed.

We were all thankful when the job was finished, giving us time to put up the tree and decorations, although the work still had to be done each day to make sure the animals were all fed and watered. Christmas turned out to be a most enjoyable time, especially sharing it with the children.

CHAPTER TEN

The New Year of 1950 found me thinking of the girls still in the hostels who knew that their Land Army days would soon be over. This made me grateful I had decided to come to the farm; at least I had been saved the heartbreak of seeing it all fold up, and seeing all my friends depart to go their separate ways, mostly back to their homes. Being scattered all over the country, it was unlikely that any of us would meet again.

It was with relief that I was told by Ron, that although I had arrived at the farm while still employed by the WAEG with my wages being paid by them, he had decided to keep me on as an ordinary farm worker in his employ as long as he could still afford to do so.

I received a letter of thanks for my service with the Land Army with best wishes for the future. On reading it, Ron said,"So that's it. I thought they would have at least given you all a medal of some kind to keep."

I thought I may have felt different not belonging to something now, but I didn't. I suppose it was because I was still doing the same sort of work.

As the weather improved, it was decided to give the shippens a spring clean. Armed with buckets and brushes we all set about doing this, and with the usual arguments about who was given the worst parts to do, the job was finally completed and tables scrubbed and placed in there ready for Pig Day.

Each year every farmer was allowed to have one of his pigs killed for his family's needs. The tables were used for jointing it up. As there were no freezers then, two farmers would share one pig between them, salting the joints into trays as a way of preserving the meat. When it was time for the other family to have their pig later in the year, they again would divide it between them. This arrangement seemed to work well, as did all the other times when farm work and machinery was shared among this tightly knit community, making a strong bond between all farming people.

While we were planting crops for the spring, I would often enter the farmhouse kitchen and find Ron in deep discussion with his wife. He told me there were to be changes in their way of farming as they had decided to increase the herd for much higher milk production, and the following year they would be introducing milking machines. The corn field would be turned into grazing land for the cattle, leaving a small field for potatoes and other crops to serve the family's needs.

Mrs Easterbrook had not enjoyed good health for some time now and was finding it increasingly difficult to cope with the work in the farmhouse, so she recruited the help of her friend May to come in at times to tackle the heavier jobs that needed doing.

It was with an amount of sadness we saw the last of the corn harvest brought in, knowing there would be no more. It had always been such a happy time for everyone.

It was a short time after all the corn had been safely stacked away I noticed Ron was unusually quiet, as if he had a lot on his mind. I soon found out when he told me that, with all the new improvements he had to make, and as there would be much less field work to do, he would not be able to employ me in the future. They had decided that May would be moving in to live with them to take over the heavier work in the farmhouse, and would be needing my room. I could see it had not been easy for him to have to tell me this, but I did understand although it was the last thing I wanted to hear. I was, however, given a full month to be able to sort out my future.

The day for me to leave arrived. I felt so sad as I packed my belongings. I saw sadness in everyone's faces too as I said my goodbyes to the place where I had shared in their laughter and tears as if I had always belonged there and been part of the family.

It seemed my life over the past five years was about to come full circle as I once again entered the profession I had left to join the Land Army – as a nurse in the Torrington Cottage Hospital, where I remained until my marriage to John the following year.

It had always seemed so easy for me to close the door on all the other aspects of my life, but those halcyon days spent mucking in with my friends and mucking out on the land, that particular door with stay forever open.

Epilogue

The house I was given after my marriage overlooked the farm where we used to go to exercise the horses. My children and their children were always welcome there and spent many enjoyable hours around the farmhouse.

In the years that followed I met up again with Flo, finding her and her family at a farm some miles away. Our friendship lasted until the present day. She eventually left the farm and married a man she was engaged to in those early days, but sadly now she has gone.

I am still in contact with the dozen or so girls from both the Torrington and Barnstaple Hostels.

Jean Bailey, one of the girls in the Torrington Hostel, later married my husband John's brother, and thus became my sister-in-law.

Moving into my new home in Bideford in 1987, my next door neighbour told me in greeting that she remembered me from all those years ago. This was Rose who I met at Instow. We are now good friends and have many chats as we tend our gardens.

After the loss of both parents, Donald took over the farm at Belle View and is still there today. His sister Margaret lives in a farmhouse a mile from there.

Vince, at the ripe old age of 80, sat with us and talked over old times when we met him in our local. He is now in a nursing home nearby.

I still get a feeling of nostalgia when passing a newly cut field or the smell of a tractor.

A few years ago I went back to Leamington Spa, stayed in Barford and visited Bromson Hill Hostel which is now a nursing home, and was made very welcome by the staff and people there. The old fireplace I stood on all those years ago was still there.